# IT'S KNOTT CRICKET

# IT'S KNOTT CRICKET

The autobiography of
**ALAN KNOTT**

MACMILLAN

*To Andy, who brought so much happiness
into our lives.*

First published 1985 by
MACMILLAN LONDON LIMITED
4 Little Essex Street London WC2R 3LF
and Basingstoke

Associated companies in Auckland, Delhi, Dublin,
Gaborone, Hamburg, Harare, Hong Kong, Johannesburg,
Kuala Lumpur, Lagos, Manzini, Melbourne, Mexico City,
Nairobi, New York, Singapore and Tokyo

Phototypeset by
Wyvern Typesetting Limited, Bristol

Printed in Great Britain by Anchor Brendon Limited,
Tiptree, Essex


British Library Cataloguing in Publication Data
Knott, Alan
    Autobiography.
    1. Knott, Alan   2. Cricket players——
    England——Biography
    I. Title
    796.35'8'0924      GV915.K/
    ISBN 0–333–38239–0

# Contents

List of Illustrations vii

Acknowledgements ix

1 Crossroads 1

2 Stretching Out 8

3 First Test 25

4 Keeping Heyday 35

5 Captain Supreme 44

6 Caribbean Trouble 56

7 Greatest Friend 66

8 Bouncers 71

9 Benefit of the Doubt 82

10 Packer 96

11 County and Test Recall 109

12 South Africa 118

13 The Changing Game 128

Appendix 1: Alan Knott's Test Wicket-keeping Record 143

Appendix 2: Alan Knott's Test Hundreds 157

Index 159

# List of Illustrations

*Between pages 22 and 23*

Dad just before taking the field for another great display behind the
    stumps.
Mum showing us how at Belvedere nets.
Always ready for a knock-around; as a youngster at Belvedere cricket
    ground.
Kent Schools cricket team.
Surrounded by friends after our wedding.
Playing for Kent at Lord's, August 1964.
Colin Cowdrey, my first captain at Kent, in great form.
Ray Illingworth at his best, during the 1969 Headingley Test.
Top-class South Africans – Sir Donald Bradman.
With three wonderful friends – Tony Greig, Dennis Amiss and
    Bernard Thomas.
Sharing a joke with groundstaff and police during the bomb scare at
    Lord's, 1973.
The incomparable Gary Sobers in full flow.
Man of the Match in Kent's successful Gillette Cup Final against
    Lancashire, 1974.
Catching Viswanath off the bowling of Geoff Arnold at Lord's in
    1974.
Part of the perfect Derek Underwood action, and two wickets that
    fell to the Knott–Underwood combination.

*Between pages 86 and 87*

An awesome sight – Dennis Lillee and Jeff Thomson.
Ian Chappell shouts congratulations to Dennis Lillee, who has had
    me caught by Ian's brother Greg.
Fending off a Thomson bouncer and cutting one high over the slips
    during the 1974–5 series.
Doug Walters pulls Bob Willis for 6 at Perth, 1974–5.

On tour – Bob Taylor keeping wicket, me at first slip and Mike Hendrick at leg slip.

The old combination – c Marsh, b Lillee.

Bob Taylor concentrating hard, wearing his favourite old gloves.

Brian Close hit by a ball from Michael Holding, John Edrich batting at Old Trafford.

Viv Richards on his way to a double century at Trent Bridge, 1976.

Dropping Wayne Daniel off John Snow at Headingley, 1976.

Batting with Tony Greig at Headingley, 1976.

Stumping Lawrence Rowe at the Oval in 1976 to establish an English wicket-keeping record.

A fantastic catch by Tony Greig during the Centenary Test at Melbourne, 1977.

Derek Randall hooks Lillee for 4.

Playing the sweep shot during my highest Test innings – 135 against Australia at Trent Bridge in 1977, in partnership with Geoff Boycott.

Catching Rick McCosker off Tony Greig's bowling . . . and Rod Marsh down the leg-side off Ian Botham.

*Between pages 118 and 119*

Kent on parade. Meeting Her Majesty the Queen at Lord's, 1980.

England celebrate the dismissal of Bacchus.

Clive Lloyd, one of the most popular players and finest captains of modern times.

Graham Gooch during his marvellous innings against the West Indies at Lord's, 1980.

Ian Botham on his way to that awe-inspiring 118 against the Australians at Old Trafford, 1981.

Catching Martin Kent off John Emburey's bowling: my 100th victim against Australia.

England's best post-war team, as selected by computer.

With Leslie Ames and Godfrey Evans – a trio of Kent and England wicket-keepers.

Paul Downton in his early Kent days.

Keeping has its ups and downs, but can be a lot of fun!

Power and style from David Gower, as Javed Miandad takes evasive action.

Mike Gatting's 216 for Middlesex against New Zealand at Lord's, 1983.

Allan Lamb on his way to a hundred in the fourth Test at Old Trafford, 1984.

Richard Hadlee – a great all-rounder.

Two great friends and colleagues -- Bob Woolmer and Dennis Amiss.

Jan and James.

With Jan and James, enjoying ourselves in Holland with Dutch friends.

# Acknowledgements

I would like to thank:

— Medway Press Services for their great help with my autobiography – especially Dudley Moore, who has been a trusted friend for many years, Stephen Brenkley and Val Wescott;

— all the friends and relations I have not mentioned in this book, including those as far afield as that small cricketing island of Australia, for putting up with me over the years;

— my Uncle Maurice and my cousin Stewart for the encouragement that they have given me;

— all those at Kent and in the professional game who have given me so many happy memories;

— the late Una Budge and the cricketing followers who gave me such great support;

— Slazenger and Gola, the two companies to which I have been contracted during my career, for their help and kindness;

— the Jack Long Trio for many entertaining evenings away from cricket;

— Danny O'Donnell, George and Elaine Popplewell, Tony Toms (and many others) for physical training, body maintenance and the stamina to write this book.

*Alan Knott*
*January 1985*

# One

# Crossroads

When I arrived home from the Centenary Test in Melbourne in the spring of 1977, my international career was at a crossroads. Certainly the question of my taking part in any future England tours abroad was very much open to doubt. Flying home from Australia, where the short tour, just two matches, had followed the winter in India and Sri Lanka, I went to chat with senior Test and County Cricket Board officials and the question of wives and families on tour cropped up in the conversation. For me that had always been a vital issue and it had come very close to persuading me not to make that winter's trip. The TCCB had said that they wanted wives to join the tour only in Sri Lanka. I had asked whether my wife Jan could join me during the time I was in India, in the middle of the tour. My view had anyway always been that it was preferable for wives to join their husbands halfway through a tour, to break it up. At first the TCCB resisted my argument, but later gave way. I felt so strongly that I was prepared to drop out of the party.

Eventually it was agreed that Jan could fly out to India halfway through the tour, and apparently the only reason why the authorities had relented was because I had been playing Test cricket for so long. Following that decision, Keith Fletcher's wife Sue was also given permission to fly out at the same time. During our conversation on the plane-trip home it was made extremely clear to me that children would not be allowed on the next tour, nor possibly would wives. There were various reasons. It was felt, for instance, that some players might not be able to afford to take their wives with them and therefore might feel out of it. The view was also expressed that the authorities would have the added responsibility of booking flights and hotels for wives, but to me that hardly seemed a difficult problem. My conclusion was that if my career took me away on tour, I could not be expected to be apart winter after winter from my wife and young son.

On my first major tour abroad after our marriage, to Australia in 1970–1, Jan had not accompanied me, and I decided never to let it happen again. The separation lasted far too long. The authorities seemed to think that if wives were on tour players would be under extra pressure, would have more worries. In my own view the reverse applies – if his wife is at home with problems, the player, thousands of miles away, is likely to worry even more. If the tour can be broken up in the middle so that husbands and wives are separated for only two months at the beginning and two at the end, it is nowhere near as intolerable as being apart for six months. If they have winters apart, the husband travelling the world, the wife staying at home and not seeing any of the places where he is playing, they can grow apart. Precisely that view had been expressed to me by Colin Cowdrey during the tour of Pakistan in 1969. We were discussing the question of touring because I was going home to get married that April. Cowdrey suggested that I should always take my wife with me on tours whenever it was possible. He felt that couples could grow apart if the wife was left at home and that they could end up by leading separate lives; it was a very unfair separation over a great length of time, winter after winter. It was good advice.

Jan had been with me in 1969–70 when I was coaching and playing in Tasmania and, having seen something of Australia then, she stayed at home during the 1970–1 tour of Down Under. It was a decision I regretted. Unfortunately I hadn't taken Cowdrey's advice on that occasion, but being on that six months' tour alone made me realize just how right he was. Since then Jan has been with me on every tour, although on the West Indies tour in 1973–4 I had to get permission for her to join me at a special time because we had just started our business. On the next tour to

Australia in 1974–5 there was the ruling that your wife couldn't stay with you in your hotel for more than twenty-one nights; nor could wives fly on the same plane when travelling. Jan in fact stayed in Australia for well over three weeks. In Adelaide there was a farcical situation when we were living in adjoining hotels. You can guess where I was every night – in the hotel next door and rushing back in the morning to have breakfast in my own hotel. Fortunately Bernard Thomas, our physio/trainer, was in charge of recording the number of nights married couples were together and he bent the rules. He took the job, I felt, because he knew he would be more flexible than anyone else. So the players had to spend time working out which nights their wives could be in the same hotel as themselves because sometimes they were away on up-country games. It could all have been organized so simply, as indeed it subsequently was during World Series Cricket, with the office administrators dealing with the whole matter.

I was probably in the minority having such a strong view about it. There is no doubt that if you start complaining you could be asking for trouble. That is especially true if you play badly. The authorities could be tempted to say: 'Oh, he always wants his wife on tour. Let's pick somebody else.' You face the risk of being labelled a bad tourist, although you could never prove that that was the authorities' view because they could always say you had lost your form. My argument stands – the way a married couple should live is together. Ironically at Adelaide I scored my first century against Australia, so travelling between hotels didn't do my cricket any harm. There were stories in the media during that tour about the presence of wives affecting players' form. The only thing that affected our form was the bowling of Dennis Lillee and Jeff Thomson.

That was the background against which my chat with TCCB officials took place. After that I just hadn't got a clue what I would do about future tours. Jan and I discussed it – concentrating our minds on how much longer I would continue playing, with particular reference to the fact that I might not be playing Test cricket any more during the winters. Our son James, then nearly two, had not come to India and when I got home he hardly realized who I was: it really did not seem fair for me to be away winter after winter. Being Christians, Jan and I prayed for guidance. We came to no definite conclusion but we felt that I should try and play on for another three English cricket seasons. But what was I going to do about the winters?

We had only been home for two days when out of the blue came a telephone call. Immediately I recognized the voice of Tony Greig; he said: 'I think I've got something that will interest you.' It was for me the first indication of Kerry Packer's plan for World Series Cricket. Tony did not go into it in any great detail but he revealed enough to gain my interest. Participation would mean playing cricket in Australia for three winters – with no restriction on wives and families, and that was the main reason why I eventually signed to play for Packer. So the telephone call from Greig was a wonderful answer to prayer. I spent two winters in Australia playing for Packer and it was the most continually competitive cricket in which I've been involved. I felt very disappointed when it was announced just before the start of the 1979 season that it would not be continuing.

Since then I haven't toured with England, having decided not to in the summer of 1979, though I came very close to going on the tour of Australia in 1979–80. Having played only the first half of that season for Kent (Paul Downton took over for the second half) as that was all I was contracted for, there were no thoughts in my mind about the winter's tour Down Under. Then, out of the blue, during the Test at Headingley, the captain Mike Brearley telephoned me at home and raised the question of my going on the tour. He asked my views about certain players who might be considered and whether I would be available myself. I asked for a fortnight to think it over. Subsequently we spoke again on the telephone and I said that I would not be available. Brearley had told me in the first call that he had discussed my situation with some of the senior England players and he said that one doubt expressed was that I had only played half the season. They had concluded though that that could be an advantage because I would have more energy and enthusiasm for the tour.

I also discussed with Brearley a matter that had astonished me. There had been a suggestion that the England players felt that if a player who had appeared in World Series Cricket was subsequently selected for England he should pay the WSC money back or put it into the England pool. Brearley assured me that that matter had been cleared up; he also said that he was sure that my family would be allowed to be with me on the tour, but despite his assurance I knew it could still cause problems. My request was that I should not be apart from them for more than four weeks. On the night of the selectors' meeting at the Victoria Sporting Club in London, Brearley, with the backing of two selectors, telephoned me to tell me that he had been asked to speak to me in a final effort to see if I would go. Even though I had earlier said no, I suggested that he phone back in an hour so that I could discuss the matter with my wife. I decided that I would make myself available after all. When Brearley rang again I told him my decision.

I wanted to go because he was captain; because he really wanted me to be in the party; and because we had got on so well during our careers. Australia is my favourite tour and it wasn't going to be too long. Later that evening Alec Bedser, the chairman of the selectors, telephoned. Naturally he was doubtful whether I really wanted to make the trip and he was checking on my decision. I told him: 'I'll go. I'll give it everything I've got.' He replied: 'Yes, I know you will.' (Sometimes Alec lives in the past, but his heart is in the right place and he really wants the players to do well. I can remember complaining about a hot, hard day in the field and Alec said that I wouldn't have complained if I had just come back from the war to play as he had done in 1946 – anything seems easier after that!)

When I went to bed that night it looked as though later that winter I would be on my way to Australia. The next morning, however, Brearley telephoned, asking, 'Has Alec rung you?' I said that he hadn't, and Brearley then told me they had decided not to take me on the tour. When Bedser rang later he confirmed: 'I'm sorry, we've decided not to take you.' After all the trouble they had taken to persuade me and all the thinking I had done before finally saying yes, I was staggered. On the other hand I didn't really mind not going; in fact, in a way I was quite relieved, because I honestly didn't know if I was looking forward to touring again.

One aspect of touring that I did enjoy was the chance it gave to see the world. Certainly I soon appreciated that and I spent a lot of time taking photographs on my sightseeing trips. On my first senior tour to the West Indies in 1968 I didn't even take a camera, but seeing John Snow with his extensive photographic equipment made me realize what I was missing. Since then I have taken my camera everywhere and have masses of slides and photographs. It is important to be aware that the opportunities to see different parts of the world might not come again. But on tour you do have to make every effort to visit places. I remember on one Indian tour we even got up at about 5 a.m. to go and see the Taj Mahal, but it was worthwhile. Some players prefer to rest, and on my early tours I didn't rush about so much trying to see places. Then I discovered how relaxing sightseeing can be. It means that you get away from cricket, whereas if you stay around the hotel, sitting by the pool, you are still very much involved. I often went on trips on my own because other players used to go off in a group, frequently undecided as to whether they were going to sightsee or not and would end up by seeing nothing. So I would make an early start, only going with other people if they genuinely wanted to sightsee. I was never very keen on sunbathing when I was playing and I remember that Geoff Boycott was very much against it because he felt that it sapped your energy. It suited me to be on my own, or perhaps with just one or two other players, because you spend so much time on tour with a group of players in dressing rooms, or hotels, or travelling in planes or buses that it is quite nice to be on your own for a change.

It was the same in the team room. In every hotel a room was set aside (in the early tours it was usually the manager's room), with drinks available, where the players could go and have a chat about the day's play. I wasn't a great believer in the idea, and I felt that too much emphasis was put on the team room. It tended to become a drinks' room and often the conversation wasn't very constructive; I've always felt that if someone has a cricket problem it is better resolved privately. Obviously I went if specifically asked, but although it was meant to be relaxing, I'm afraid I didn't find it so. I could never understand why the players wanted to be together every hour of the day. It was a great shame that people seemed afraid of being away from the company of a group.

Of all the places I have visited, California and Hawaii are the ones I would choose to live in. Tasmania and New Zealand are high up on my list of favourite places, along with Bermuda, which is fantastically beautiful, Hong Kong, where I loved the excitement, and Sydney, which I think is the second prettiest city in the world, beaten only by San Francisco.

I am glad that I have been able to see most of these places with my family. Jan has been with me to every country apart from two, while James has travelled with us to such an extent that by the time he was five years old he had been round the world twice. It was a joy to see how well he adapted to all the new experiences – living in hotels and meeting so many people of different nationalities never seemed to worry him. Travelling must have contributed a great deal to his friendly, outgoing personality.

James will have a go at any sport – an attitude that applies to everything he does in life. He has stacks of energy and it is a great thrill for me that when he comes to a cricket match he is always willing to join in with the hordes of young boys who play on the other side of the boundary ropes. If he eventually displays the talent to be a professional sportsman I will not dissuade him.

Indeed, when I retire I hope to keep up my interest in the game by coaching, thereby helping to develop the talent of youngsters generally. It affords much satisfaction and is very rewarding when, after many patient coaching sessions, you see the happiness on the face of a young boy who, having started without any body and arm co-ordination, has learnt to bowl straight. As a coach perhaps I will be able to supply some of the encouragement and instruction that I was so glad to receive when I was a boy.

# Two

# Stretching Out

Should I stay on at school to try to qualify for teacher-training college or leave to take up a career as a professional cricketer? That was the decision that faced me as a sixteen-year-old at the end of the summer term of 1962 at Northumberland Heath Secondary Modern School, near Erith.

Cricket was my choice. I had obtained three O-levels and needed another two to go on to college, which I think I would have enjoyed. Staying on for the extra year and being able to play only part-time while at college, however, could have jeopardized my cricket career. Many young players today spend three years at university or college before returning to their counties full-time. There have been exceptions, but they face the possibility of losing out at cricket. I was playing for England at twenty-one but if I had gone to college I might not have been a Test cricketer until I was twenty-five – and I was past my peak as a wicket-keeper by then. Paul Downton was recalled as England's wicket-keeper in 1984 but he could have missed out in Test cricket because he spent three years at Exeter University.

Fortunately my father advised me to play cricket rather than stay at school. He was a very talented cricketer himself and I respected him tremendously, valuing his opinion not just because he was my father. He played club cricket until he was

fifty and probably could have played the game professionally. I
owe him a great deal for my successful career. He was a fantastic
encourager. He always treated me as if I was going to play
professional sport. He never pushed me but his encouragement
gave me confidence in my ability. He had some good sayings and
one which really made me think and try 100 per cent every time I
was playing or practising was: 'Son, remember there's always
somebody better than you.'

It is wonderful to look back to those days of cricket in the street
with my brother, when a neighbour would hold on to our tennis
ball after it had gone into their garden for the umpteenth time
until my mother knocked on the door and asked for it back in her
own persuasive way. Mum must take much credit for making
sure that our practice never finished until night came. We would
quite often then continue indoors in our hallway with Dad, my
older brother Francis and myself fulfilling the batting, wicket-
keeping or first-slip roles. The wicket-keeper would throw the
ball against the wall and the rebound was treated as if the ball had
been bowled, with the batsman using a cricket stump as his bat.
Mum was very good in not worrying about damage to the hall,
just occasionally asking us to stop for a tea break. It was all great
training and such fun that we never wanted to stop.

Dad certainly inspired in us the fun of sport and just watching
him play was a lesson in itself. From the age of four I watched him
keeping wicket for Erith Technical College Association. Then as a
ten-year-old I was scorer for the club's first eleven, and a few
years later I played for the second eleven. I had played for the first
team at Belmont Primary School – I was a fast bowler then – and
was in the first team as a first-year boy at my secondary school. I
played representative cricket at school level for North-West Kent,
Kent, South of England and England. At club level I played for
my father's team, and one game for Dartford, whose home
ground, Hesketh Park, is one of Kent CCC's grounds.

Those early days of school and club cricket were vital for the
support I received. I always remember with affection the kindness of my cricket and history master Jack Morris, for taking me to
the nets at Eltham Baths. He must have been quite a teacher too
because he got me through my history O-level first time. Players
and officials at the Erith Technical College Association, later
known as Belvedere, studied every department of my game and

gave each one the opportunity to blossom. Just before I turned professional, Kent County Cricket Club suggested that I should play for Blackheath, which was the best side in the area in those days. Blackheath's players continued to encourage me, as had those at Belvedere, and I was fortunate to play with two cricketers who turned out briefly for Kent – Mike Olten, off-spinner and batsman, and Jimmy Melville, an opening bowler. They helped me to prepare for what lay ahead on the county circuit. Those school and club games were really great, and I looked forward to each match. Now perhaps when I am not relishing the thought of taking part in a county match the following day, having played twenty or so days continually in the middle of August, it does me good to think back and remember how those fellow club and school players would love to be in my position.

One schools game always stands out in my memory. I was fourteen, playing for the South of England Schools at Cranleigh on the ground overlooked by the home of Peter May, the current chairman of the England selectors. Very small for my age and wearing short trousers, I knocked on the dressing-room door. When he saw me, the manager said, 'What do you want, son?' I replied that I was there to play! Some of my colleagues in that schools game were later to become opponents on the county circuit – Geoff Arnold (Surrey and Sussex), Roy Wills (Northamptonshire) and Peter Graves (Sussex) – while Derek Underwood went on to become a Kent colleague.

My father was one of the old school whose view was that wicket-keepers didn't need to bat. He hadn't batted much himself, going in low down the order. One of the most important lessons he taught me was never to give up but to carry on in the same way because things would come right in the end – advice which was echoed from other sources later in my career. He also stressed that, as far as keeping your place in a team was concerned, possession was nine points of the law. He qualified that by saying if you were a wicket-keeper or a goalkeeper there was only one position in the team for you, so if you got in and did your job well you had a reasonable chance of keeping your place. He contended that great things came in small packages, which I took as an encouraging remark, although I think the day of the taller wicket-keeper could well come. With fast bowlers dominating the modern game and wicket-keepers invariably stood well back, a tall 'keeper can move and dive so much further, covering more ground to reach short-pitched deliveries flying high to, or even over, the 'keeper as batsmen get top edges cutting or hooking. Already we have seen some tall wicket-keepers at the top level – Richie Robinson from Australia, who kept superbly in WSC, and the brilliant South African Ray Jennings, who is over six feet.

My father never threw praise away and that was probably good for me. He used to say, 'You'll never be as good as me, son' – which I remember believing. He has seen me playing county games and the odd Test, and he seemed disappointed after I joined World Series Cricket, fearing that I wouldn't play for England again. There was nothing much for him to follow if I was playing in Australia every winter. Deep down I think he has enjoyed watching my career and he was probably sad that he never played professional sport himself. He understood my job, playing cricket as a career, but couldn't appreciate the effects of the other less enjoyable aspects like travelling and living in hotels. Nor did he ever know what a difficult task it was to keep wicket for six hours or more a day.

I had been involved with the Kent club since I first went, at the age of twelve, to the indoor nets at Eltham, a path trodden by so many of the county's players. Claude Lewis, now the Kent scorer, but then the coach, felt that it might be hard for me to open both batting and bowling, as I did at school, where I bowled quick. He suggested I should switch to spin bowling. I used to bowl both leg- and off-spin, an accomplishment which went against me in one early second-eleven match at Worcester. On a really plumb wicket I toiled away with off-spin until my finger split and bled. I reported my injury to Colin Page, the skipper, who merely replied, 'You had better switch to leg-breaks then.' It was Lewis who had taught me the art of spin bowling. He was a terrific coach, understanding and encouraging. He knew all about spin bowling and how batsmen should play it. Facing such a high-class bowler in the nets was a tremendous experience for a youngster.

Eventually Kent wanted me to join their staff. The county's secretary/manager at that time – Les Ames, the former England and Kent wicket-keeper and batsman – came to our house to discuss the matter with my father. So during the summers of 1961 and 1962 I spent the school holidays as a semi-professional with

Kent. My first games were for the county's club and ground side at Aylesford – Brian Luckhurst was the skipper – and then for the second eleven on the old Nore Command ground at Chatham against the Royal Engineers. On my debut for the county's second eleven in a championship match I didn't keep wicket. The captain, Derek Ufton, who played cricket for Kent and soccer for Charlton and England, was behind the stumps. The match was against Northamptonshire and my first victim when I was called on to bowl off-breaks was Malcolm Scott, with the last ball of my first over. Indeed Les Ames suggested in those early days that I should concentrate on my bowling. I have always liked to bowl but without the advantage of height it is difficult to get more bounce off the wicket for catches to carry to close fielders.

My first full season on the staff was 1963. Tony Catt was the first-eleven wicket-keeper and in the second eleven I shared those duties with Ufton, bowling thirty-five overs of off-breaks and taking 2 for 95 in the games when I was not behind the stumps. In twenty-five innings I totalled 420 runs with a top score of 56 in the last game of the season against Sussex at Broadstairs. Some of my most regular colleagues in the second eleven, skippered as I have said by Colin Page, were Derek Ufton, John Prodger, David Constant, now a Test match umpire, David Sayer, Norman Graham and David Baker, a leg-spinner who later moved to Nottinghamshire. The young players, not then on the staff, who had second-eleven games included Alan Ealham, Richard Burnett, whose grandfather was the legendary Frank Woolley, and Frank Ames, a cousin of Les Ames.

In 1964 I kept wicket regularly in the second eleven, Ufton having left the staff to become a soccer manager, and I nearly made my first-team debut at Tunbridge Wells. I did in fact report to the ground with a chance of playing but in the event I was not chosen. So my first chance in the senior side came at Folkestone on 27 June that year in the three-day game against Cambridge University, then captained by Mike Brearley, who kept wicket in that match. I had been given the exciting news the previous day at Dartford where I was in the second-eleven side against Surrey. The news made me a little bit apprehensive. Stuart Leary, who had digs near my home in Erith, and was my soccer hero at Charlton, was in the Kent side and he drove me and my father to the ground.

That University side included Richard Hutton, son of Sir Leonard, Tony Windows, who subsequently played for Gloucestershire, and Roy Kerslake, who went on to play for Somerset. The University batted first and I did not have long to wait for my first catch – Brearley's opening partner Daniels off David Sayer. It was a diving effort. As I caught it in my right hand the ball dropped out but I managed to hold it in both hands as it came down. I picked up two more catches in the innings but had to wait longer for my first runs at senior level, for I was number nine in the order. When I got in, my first ball was from Graham Pritchard, later to play for Essex, who had become a good friend when we were together in the Kent second eleven. It was a slow full toss which I am sure was deliberately bowled to enable me to get off the mark in my debut. Looking back on it, I suppose I should have pushed it away for a single. Instead I was so tense that I hit it square through the covers for four. Hutton, who subsequently played for Yorkshire and now lives near Tunbridge Wells – he often pops in when Kent play there – was quite annoyed. 'Is this first-class cricket?' he shouted. Hutton was involved in another incident towards the end of the match when we were chasing 267 to win (we got them with three wickets to spare). I was 9 not out at the end and in the closing overs Hutton was wasting time, running in to bowl from the sightscreen. Brearley became very cross and told him to complete the over more quickly. He then bowled off a couple of paces and conceded more runs than he might have done. I was to learn that Richard Hutton was a very funny man with a dry sense of humour – like father, like son.

I stayed in the side for my championship debut – against Leicestershire – in the second match of Folkestone week. I didn't bat in the first innings, was not out again on 13 in the second, and held three catches, all off Sayer, when Leicestershire batted first. I missed a chance to stump Clive Inman before he had scored and he went on to get a century. In their second innings I took my first ever championship catch off Derek Underwood, who had enjoyed such a remarkably successful debut season in 1963, at eighteen the youngest ever player to take 100 wickets in his first season. Catt returned to the side for the next eight games. Back in the second eleven I made an 81 and an 82 not out, at that time my highest ever Kent scores, and was recalled for first-team duty against Northamptonshire at Wellingborough on 8 August. I

stayed in then for the rest of the season, which included the
match against the Australians at Canterbury.

How the pattern of tourist matches against the counties has
changed over the years. In the old days county players wanted to
play against the tourists – it was an important occasion. Now
players are not unhappy if they miss that game, because it gives
them a rest. If they do play, it is quite a relaxation from championship cricket, with no thoughts directed to bonus points and
bowling rates. Nor do these tourist matches appeal so much to
spectators, who have seen so many of them in the flesh, playing
for English counties, or being very extensively covered on television. Players too have encountered them on the county circuit.
Kent, in my early days, seemed to have the wrong approach to
the tourists' games, feeling almost obliged to give them practice
and to play in a very friendly and co-operative spirit. The
impression was that Colin Cowdrey, then the Kent captain,
would toss up, and the tourists could pretty well do as they
wished. My view then was that such matches should be treated
as proper games – in Australia I was to find that all our games
against the State sides were like Test matches.

Certainly I enjoyed my first encounter with the Australians at
Canterbury, playing against such heroes as Bill Lawry, Peter
Burge, Norman O'Neill and their great wicket-keeper Wally
Grout, who caught me as I pushed forward to Ian Redpath. The
Aussies won that game by eight wickets, despite a century for us
in each innings by Peter Richardson, who frequently skippered
the side in the absence of Cowdrey on Test duty. During that
game I experienced for the first time one of the pranks for which
Richardson was famous. He suddenly stopped play while he was
batting and asked the umpires to go over to the commentary box
and ask Jim Swanton not to speak so loudly. Swanton, later to
become a member of the Kent committee and the club's
president, got out of it very well by remarking on the air, 'There
seems to be a problem with one of our lights.' It was obviously
prearranged by Richardson, because we were all sitting in the
dressing room waiting to see how Swanton got out of an awkward situation.

That same season at Cardiff, Richardson played a joke on
another commentator, Wilf Wooller, who was also the Welsh
county's secretary. It was John Prodger's birthday and as he

walked to the wicket we all sang 'Happy Birthday' and the Welsh crowd readily joined in. It was the Cambridge cap worn by Prodger which attracted Wooller's attention. He came to our dressing room to ask Richardson why he was wearing it. He doubted whether Prodger was a blue but Richardson, tongue in cheek, convinced him that he was, giving imaginary details of how long he had been at Cambridge and at which college. Eventually Wooller agreed with Richardson, saying, 'Yes, yes, you're right,' and returned to the commentary box with information which was of course completely false. Jim Presdee meanwhile had entered into the birthday spirit by delivering a full toss to Prodger, who pushed it away for a single. He couldn't fail because everyone was back on the boundary. That sort of thing rarely happens today.

Richardson, who played thirty-four times for England, mainly before he joined Kent from Worcestershire in 1959, was a clever captain and would have enjoyed tremendous success in modern cricket. An attacking leader and an exhilarating cricketer, today's game, with the chase for bonus points and for victory in the last innings, and particularly the limited-overs competitions, would have suited him ideally. He was the best player of the sweep shot that I have seen; watching and listening to him helped me to add that shot to my repertoire.

I have always enjoyed the challenge of playing on turning wickets against left-arm spinners – probably a result of the early tuition and practice that I received from Claude Lewis – and I have never agreed with the theory that you shouldn't sweep against the spin. The sweep is probably my favourite shot, used mainly on bad wickets when the ball is turning. If the bowler is maintaining a good length then that is the ideal time to sweep. If you play forward with a straight bat the ball is an awkward distance away from your defensive stroke. When you sweep, however, you meet the pitch of the ball on the half volley because the bat is way out in front of you and parallel to the ground. I always believe that on bad wickets it is much safer to sweep the left-arm spinner than to try to drive a ball that is spinning away from you and risk edging a catch to wicket-keeper or slip. With the sweep there is less chance of an edge, but if there is it should be a top edge and the ball should fly safely over the wicket-keeper's and slips' heads. The art of sweeping is not to hit the ball too hard and not to panic. Be prepared to hit the ball with any part of the bat from the toe up to the splice, or in the last resort even with the gloves if it will mean preventing an l.b.w. decision. The danger ball for l.b.w. is the one that is going to pitch just before the front pad. Don't panic, stay low, stretch well forward and gently sweep the ball before it pitches. If you hurry the shot, hitting the ball too hard, the top edge can send it flying into the hands of the deep-leg-side fielder, but play it gently with more touch and control and it won't go to hand. There's an opportunity to vary the shot from wide mid-wicket to as fine as just past the wicket-keeper. Because the rules state that there can be only two fielders behind square leg, you have the added advantage of a good area into which the ball can be played and runs accumulated. When sweeping, keep your head still and your eyes on the ball: some players tend to turn their heads away, thinking that they would top-edge the ball into their faces, but if you look at the ball and it is coming towards your face, your natural reactions automatically make you move your head clear. If your eyes are turned away and you can't see the ball there is a far greater chance of it hitting you on the head.

One of the left-arm spinners I have respected most over the years has been Phil Edmonds. What an amazing career he has had. He has so much talent as bowler, batsman and fielder that it is incredible that he has not always been Underwood's number two on tour or the leading left-arm spinner when Underwood has not been available.

During my first games for Kent towards the end of the 1964 season, I had been most impressed by another young player, Ted Fillary, whom I rate as one of the two best leg-spinners I've ever seen – the West Indian Willie Rodriguez was the other. Fillary, an Oxford blue, would almost certainly have been on an England tour as a leg-spinner and useful batsman if he had continued in the game. At Dover that year in an innings defeat by Yorkshire, for whom Ray Illingworth had scored 135 and taken 14 for 101 in the match, Fillary had carried his bat through our second innings. In the next match we were at Lord's and on his way to the ground Fillary was followed in his car by four lads on motorcycles. When he stopped at traffic lights they pulled him out of the car and beat him up. He arrived in the dressing room with blood all over his bruised face but ended the game with happier memories as he bowled Middlesex out in their second innings, taking 5 for 52 and enabling Kent to win by nine wickets. It was a belter of a wicket and the only bowlers who were going to succeed were top-class pacemen or leg-spinners. I had kept to Fillary since our schooldays but couldn't always pick whether he was to bowl a leg-break or a googly, so as a precaution he always signalled his intentions. He used to pretend that the signal was to tug his sweater but in fact it was the way he went round his marker – anti-clockwise for the leg-break, clockwise for the googly. On an Association of Kent Cricket Clubs tour to the Midlands one of the opposing batsmen fell into the trap of watching Fillary tugging his sweater. Eventually the batsman charged down the wicket anticipating the googly, but it was the leg-break and he was stumped.

At the start of the 1965 season when Tony Catt had gone to live and work in South Africa, leaving me as the only wicket-keeper on the staff, I asked Mr Ames if I merited a rise. My salary was less than £500, and that's how it stayed because Kent said I was too young to justify an increase.

The previous winter my cricket education had been greatly helped by a tour to the West Indies with the International Cavaliers, a side composed of invited county players, sponsored by Carreras-Rothmans. With only a limited experience in the first-class game I considered myself very fortunate to be on that tour, my first abroad. Other young players on the tour included Keith Fletcher, Ron Headley and Jackie Hampshire, and it provided us with a wonderful experience and the chance to play with or against some of the world's top players. The Cavaliers party also included Colin Cowdrey, Jim Laker, Tom Graveney, Trevor Bailey and Fred Trueman. Trueman had been a hero of mine since my days as an opening bowler.

For me the main interest was to see Godfrey Evans, one of my predecessors in the Kent and England sides, in action. He had retired from first-class cricket then but watching him in action 'live' for the first time made me wonder how great he must have been at his peak. His energy, strength and enthusiasm made a real impact on me. He had the patience to wait for his chance to come yet he was a wicket-keeper who looked to attack every ball, especially for stumpings, and he displayed an aggressive attitude in diving full length to catch or take. He was prepared to go for

anything. That was one of the most important lessons he taught
me – never to hesitate. He would encourage you continually,
keeping you going, particularly if things went wrong. You might
drop the easiest catch of your career but off the next ball you could
take one of your best ever. Incidentally, Evans's advice was really
brought home to me some years later against Glamorgan at
Gravesend when I dropped three catches in three balls, two off
Alan Brown and one off Alan Dixon. Evans was always living for
the next ball, for the next moment in life. His strength was quite
staggering. I remember one evening he grabbed 'Butch' White
(the Hampshire and England fast bowler, and a pretty big man)
by the elbows and lifted him up until his head was just touching
the ceiling. It was an amazing sight.

That winter in the Caribbean provided my first opportunity of
seeing Gary Sobers 'live'. He played a truly fantastic innings at
Sabina Park, hitting one delivery from Hampshire so hard over
mid-off that if the ball had not crashed into the stand who knows
where it would have finished – it was still on the way up. Sobers I
came to appreciate over the years as easily the best all-rounder of
my time and the best batsman – even above the phenomenal Viv
Richards. He played absolutely straight and hit the ball extremely
hard, always appearing very much in command of the bowling.
He was a fantastic all-round fielder, particularly brilliant at
backward short leg to the right-handed batsman, and taking
many miraculous catches. He was the greatest swing bowler I
have ever seen. He swung the ball very late and was deceptively
quick. He could spin the ball too, but after shoulder problems he
couldn't disguise the 'chinaman' so effectively. Playing for the
West Indies at Canterbury in 1966 he spun Kent to defeat, taking
9 for 49. Against the Rest of the World at Edgbaston in 1970 I was
concentrating so hard trying to read his spin that I was speaking
my thoughts as he came into bowl. I would quietly say 'Googly'
or whatever, and it earned me a mild rebuke from the master. He
couldn't have heard me but someone must have told him because
he was a bit upset that a batsman should be calling out what sort
of ball was being delivered. I was very sorry to upset him, but it
was purely that I was so tensed up trying to work it all out.

During that tour I received one of the best pieces of advice I
have ever had. Jackie Hendricks, the West Indies wicket-keeper,
told me: 'Wicket-keepers are very rarely selected for England

unless they can bat.' It was a remark that stuck in my mind and that it has served me well to remember. I think young wicket-keepers should be encouraged as much as possible to be front-line batsmen too. Often they are not; perhaps we still live a little bit in the old days when wicket-keepers didn't have to bat. Now when Test cricket is won so much by pace-bowling it can help to have a wicket-keeper who is also a batsman, and this has been an important feature of the great West Indies sides of recent years with such players as Deryck Murray, David Murray and now Jeff Dujon. It enables them to play the extra pace bowler.

I met my wife Jan while I was working temporarily for Associated Portland Cement Manufacturers at Northfleet. While I was on the four-week tour to the West Indies Jan had joined the company as an assistant secretary and had the job of sending my wages each week to my parents' home. She knew nothing about cricket; she thought we were all amateurs who had full-time jobs, and that mine was with APCM. I returned from the tour and met her for the first time when she brought the daily milk ration round to the laboratory where I was working. Later I popped into her office and asked her out.

My wife's family have always been a tremendous help. I met them for the first time on a cold night in March 1965 over an evening meal at their home in Northfleet. Jan's brothers are all much bigger than me and much quicker eaters – mind you, I'm extremely slow – and I was so busy talking to Jan's parents for the first time that when I eventually put my knife and fork down indicating that I had finished, the boys left the table in a flash. It was a green light for them to collect their desserts. Jan's mum and dad have been a great support to us and have looked after James on many occasions. Without that it would have been impossible for Jan and myself to be together so much, either on tour or away from home in this country. A regular England cricketer can be away from home on average three-quarters of each year, so those extra periods snatched together are very important. Jan's younger brother Graham, who is in the RAF, is a semi-professional sportsman: he tells me he works when he's given time off from rugby, tennis, soccer and cricket. He noticed on a visit to Trent Bridge to watch Kent in a Sunday game that most of the side were overweight – he must have a keen eye, for since that season we have been weighed in during pre-season training and then regularly throughout the summer. Brian, Jan's older brother, at the same time as following my cricket career has also encouraged me in my business life. He has his own business, Kwik-Strip, in the Medway towns, but before that he was a top man in acoustics and has fitted home stereo systems for such famous cricketers as Derek Underwood and Basil D'Oliveira.

During my first full season in the Kent side, in 1965, I aggravated a pre-season groin injury during the match against Middlesex at Lord's. I was sent to see Bill Tucker, one of the leading orthopaedic surgeons in the country, who was very much involved in sports injuries. He examined me in the Royal Homeopathic Hospital in London and was not terribly worried about the injury, being more concerned about the lack of mobility, especially in my hip area. He was very surprised about it, having discovered it when he put me into mobilizing positions. He has not been the only person to think that way over the years; the current Kent medical advisers, our orthopaedic surgeon Reg Jones and physiotherapist Bob Chappell, were surprised too. The make-up of ligaments, tendons and muscles, or even the body's chemistry generally, can make some people extremely supple while others are stiff. My stiffness problems started when I was sixteen. Such things as getting on to the pillion of my brother's motorcycle were less easy after that.

Before that injury in 1965 I had done a lot of stretching exercises and Bill Tucker emphasized that I must continue with them. He warned that if I didn't I would be very lucky to play after the age of thirty because generally mobility decreases and I would not be able to play sport at a high level. He feared that in years to come I might develop an osteo-arthritic condition, and I went back to him annually for several years to be stretched under anaesthetic so that my limbs were totally relaxed for the mobility exercises. He set guidelines for my pre-breakfast exercise routines during the 1970–1 tour of Australia which Bernard Thomas, England's physio/trainer, built upon and over the years I have developed my own patterns of exercises, on and off the field, in consultation with the different people who have helped me with fitness. Since 1972 I have done even more exercising on the field. I came to accept the way I was – you have to, whether you suffer mild pain or lack of mobility, and play within the limits it imposes. It is something I have tried not to talk about publicly until now because I was sure that, if I had, the stories would have been blown up out of all proportion.

In 1965 I was worried about how I would survive in the first-class game as a 'keeper. I even talked to a doctor and great friend, Max Landau, later to be my benefit committee chairman, about the effect wicket-keeping might have on my hips and was wondering about concentrating on batting and bowling, for which you don't need the same type of mobility. It was still early in my professional career and not too late for me to revert to being a bowler. This problem was the main reason why I went in 1967 to train with Charlton Football Club at the Valley – to try and improve my mobility. Years earlier, as it happens, I had been sent for a trial with Crystal Palace by former Charlton winger Charlie Revell. Unfortunately I never heard anything further. I played on the wing or at inside forward and had a spell in the reserve side at Tooting and Mitcham when Derek Ufton was manager. My career as a footballer ended at the age of seventeen when it was clear that I would never be good enough to play professionally, so I decided to concentrate solely on cricket. Kent suggested that if that were so I shouldn't play football: they were definitely influenced by soccer injuries to Alan Brown and Brian Luckhurst. Training at Charlton taught me the importance of fitness in sport. Bob Stokoe was the manager then at the Valley and one of my happiest sporting moments was to see Bob, in 1973, running on to the pitch at Wembley after his team, Sunderland, had won the FA Cup.

In 1970, before the last Test against the Rest of the World, I had terrible pains behind the knee, which accounted for those pre-breakfast exercises with Bernard Thomas in Australia the follow-ing winter. This ended my rooming arrangements with Geoff Boycott which had begun in the West Indies in 1968. In Australia I needed an alarm clock, which I used to put on the floor under a pillow so that it would be less likely to wake Geoff. Then I would sneak out to do the exercises in Bernard's room. However, my early morning routine occasionally woke up my room-mate and I switched rooms to share with Peter Lever, now Lancashire's coach, who said, 'There's no way you're going to have an alarm clock in this room,' and it disappeared, never to be found again. There was nearly an unfortunate sequel, for on one of the days of the Adelaide Test we overslept and, arriving at the ground late, we were only just ready in time to play.

I was desperate not to lose mobility, otherwise I would lose much of the technical requirement for a wicket-keeper. As it was I was handicapped by my lack of hamstring mobility. A wicket-keeper needs to be able to take the ball with legs as straight as is comfortable in order to have the correct 'giving' room – in other words, so that he can bring his hands back a very similar distance every time, at whatever height the ball may be. My hamstrings meant that I had to bend my knees, and the 'giving' room available was therefore dependent on the height at which the ball was taken. I would much rather not have had to do as many exercises as I have done, but they have been essential for me. You see people gliding around like ballet dancers and I would love to have been like that. Instead I find that at least half an hour's stretching exercise is necessary every morning when I get out of bed. Other people jump up straight away, draw back the curtains and they're ready for the day. Whatever form of exercise I take part in I like to loosen up first, even playing with my son in the garden. On the other hand, I have seen so many sportsmen take risks in charity and benefit games, even up-country games on tour, by not loosening up properly and then pay the penalty with injury.

After I have retired from first-class cricket I will always take the same precautions when I am involved in any sporting activity. What those activities will be I don't know. It could be a training programme, being involved in the gymnasium that my wife and I have at Herne Bay, or maybe swimming. I played squash regularly for a couple of years but I didn't enjoy it a great deal. Another game I have given up is golf, because I found it didn't provide enough exercise for me and although I played quite often in benefit and charity matches – I used a five-wood for almost every shot when I was not putting – it was not one of my favourite games. I enjoyed table tennis in my younger days; I used to play in the top division of the North-West Kent League until I started touring in 1967 and it certainly helped my reactions tremendously. I might go back to it in a less competitive form, possibly practising with Alan Ealham, a very fine player.

In 1966 Kent finished fourth in the championship, their highest position since 1947, and the winter was to be an important one for

*Above: Always ready for a knock-around; as a youngster at Belvedere cricket ground.*

*Right: Dad just before taking the field for another great display behind the stumps.*

*Below: Mum showing us how at Belvedere nets. I am keeping wicket and my brother Francis is at slip.*

*Above: Captain of Kent Schools cricket team. Graham Johnson, who was to become a county colleague for twenty years, is second from my left in the front row.*

*Below: Surrounded by friends after our wedding. In the foreground from the world of professional sport are (left to right): Charlton footballer Brian Kinsey, Brian Luckhurst, Claude Lewis, Pat Pocock, Norman Graham, best man John Prodger, Graham Johnson, Alan Dixon, David Sayer, Colin Page, Mike Denness and Alan Brown.*

*Above: Playing for Kent at Lord's, August 1964. Very early days – sleeves rolled up, white gloves and no floppy hat. John Prodger and Colin Cowdrey seem certain it was out. (Sport & General)*

*Below left: Colin Cowdrey, my first captain at Kent, in great form. (Patrick Eagar)*

*Below right: Ray Illingworth at his best, bowling under pressure during the 1969 Headingley Test. Clive Lloyd is the victim, c Knott, b Illingworth. (The Photo Source/Central Press)*

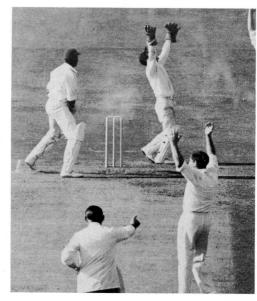

When the Rest of the World team came to England in 1970 I had the opportunity to play in an international context against such top-class South Africans as Barry Richards (left) and Eddie Barlow, who clean-bowled me for a duck at Headingley on his way to 4 wickets in 5 balls.
(Left: Patrick Eagar;
below: Sport & General)

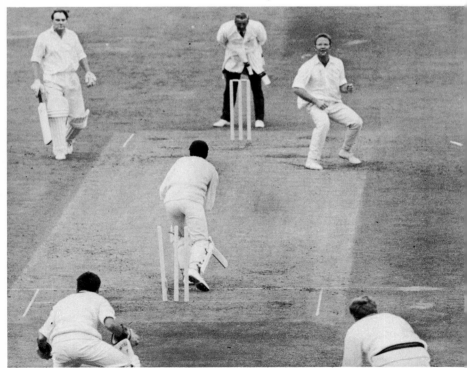

*Above: Listening to one of the greats – Sir Donald Bradman, just after we had regained the Ashes in 1970–1.*

*Below: With three wonderful friends – Tony Greig, Dennis Amiss and Bernard Thomas – on a cold day at Lord's before heading off on tour.*

*Above: Sharing a joke with groundstaff and police during the bomb scare at Lord's in the third Test against the West Indies, 1973. (Patrick Eagar)*

*Left: The incomparable Gary Sobers in full flow in that series. (Patrick Eagar)*

*Above: I was lucky enough to be made Man of the Match in Kent's successful Gillette Cup Final against Lancashire in 1974. I think Jack Bailey (left) is wondering whether the wrong person has received the award!* (Patrick Eagar)

*Below: Catching Viswanath off the bowling of Geoff Arnold at Lord's in 1974. I took more Test dismissals off Geoff's bowling than any other bowler. Perfect backing up by Keith Fletcher at first slip. I was very lucky to play so much cricket throughout my career with such fine people as Geoff and Keith.* (Patrick Eagar)

*Part of the perfect Derek Underwood action
(right), and two wickets that fell to the
Knott–Underwood combination –
thanks, Deadly.
(Right: Jan Traylen;
below: Patrick Eagar)*

me because I was selected for the five weeks' tour of Pakistan by an MCC under-25 team, under the managership of Les Ames and the captaincy of Mike Brearley.

Brearley was perfectly at home on that continent. He dressed in their style, seemed to eat anything put in front of him, mixed perfectly with everyone and of course played and captained brilliantly. In fact he became known as 'The King'. He did have his faults – he was not a natural athlete and struggled with his running, because he was very upright with high knee movements and looked as if he was running on the spot rather than forward. He could sometimes be moody but he had the ability not to let his moods last long, clouding his judgement. On that tour he showed great talent as a batsman and I suppose he never really fulfilled that promise. He became over-planned and robotic in his style, which stopped his natural flair coming through. He likes to think positively: 'Think wickets', was one of his great statements during a hard day in the field. If getting the greatest happiness out of life is a matter of loving people, then one of Mike's outstanding qualities is that no matter whom he meets he takes an interest in them. This may have led him to his present vocation, psychotherapy, but another thing that may have nudged him on his way is that over the years he seems to have been searching for the real Mike Brearley. I only hope that if he does find him he will not lose the variety of great qualities we know – sparkling and boyish on the one hand combined with a great calm and understanding on the other. That quick, humorous mind is greatly missed in the game.

I was thrilled at the prospect of my first official overseas tour. It proved very arduous as there were seven first-class fixtures packed into the thirty-four days – and I played in all of them.

On that tour I had my first experience of playing against Majid Khan, who with his floppy hat and yellowing pads must have influenced my own views of dressing for comfort rather than style. He certainly was a player to follow and I was fortunate to play alongside him in World Series Cricket. He was the charming 'Mr Casual' of cricket.

The game against North Zone at Peshawar will stay in my mind because in it I scored my maiden first-class century, 101. My opening partner, Brearley, went on to score an unbeaten 312 in the day's play.

It was the sort of trip that can do nothing but help a young cricketer, acquainting him with different environments, playing conditions and pitches, and generally getting him acclimatized to the idea of touring. If finance and the lack of crowds didn't count against under-25 tours, I would love to see them back in operation.

# *Three*

# First Test

Seven catches in a Test debut – that was the memorable start to my England career, which has spanned 100 games, five of which were against the Rest of the World and eventually not counted as Tests. Yet my first catch in the second of the three-Test series against Pakistan at Trent Bridge in 1967 could have been more comfortable. Billy Ibadulla was the victim, Ken Higgs the bowler, and the ball swung late. Passing very close to the body it was hidden from my vision until almost the last moment. I was very relieved to catch it because I hadn't really sighted the ball that well. I was not 100 per cent certain that the batsman had nicked it but everybody appealed and he was given out.

It was an exciting moment. Indeed it had been an exciting four days since I had heard the news of my selection: on the Sunday as I was travelling to play for Kent I heard the England team announced on the car radio. I had received hints that I might be in the side but because of my experience the previous season I was a little bit apprehensive about getting too keyed up: the year before it had been suggested on the grapevine that I might be picked for the last Test against the West Indies at the Oval. On the Sunday when the side was announced I was playing in a club match in Essex for my wife's boss and slipped away to the car to listen to the radio. It was John Murray, however, who was named as the wicket-keeper and he scored a century in that Oval Test, against the renowned pace-bowling combination of Wes Hall and Charlie Griffith. During the winter Murray went to Barbados, playing for a World XI, and batted marvellously again against Hall and Griffith in an innings the locals rated as one of the best ever at their Kensington Oval. In the 1967 season, he played in all three Tests against India and in the first against Pakistan. But Murray didn't have the best of times that summer and my chance came.

There is quite a feeling about winning your England colours. Everyone's thoughts probably echo those of Eric Russell, who just before the start of his first Test was heard to say, 'They can't take it away from you, old boy. It's Eric Russell – Middlesex and England.' Fortunately I was well equipped to deal with the problem of pre-match nerves because I had been talking to my local GP, Dr Lobo, a keen Indian cricket fan, and he said, 'You might find yourself playing in a Test match one day and if you're nervous the thing to take is Kaolin Morphine.' I remember taking it on that first day at Trent Bridge and I have repeated the dose ever since – on every day of a Test match in which I've played. It really does relax you and calms the butterflies. You tend to be more nervous the more Test cricket you play. In the first few games you seem to float through reasonably well because nobody is expecting you to do anything fantastic. You score a nice little 20 and they say 'Well done', but later in your career they are hoping you will hit a hundred – there is more pressure on you then from everybody: the media, the public and the administrators. People's nerves show in different ways. The signs which betray me when I'm waiting to bat are that my hands go icy cold, my face glows and quite often I feel sleepy. People say, 'Oh, he can't be nervous, look at him yawning and dozing off.' How wrong they are.

Brian Close was my first Test captain. Aggressive and absolutely fearless, he was a very warm man and made me feel at home immediately. He spoke to you as if you were part of the scenery, confirming what I had always felt when playing against him on the county circuit, that he was a very friendly person. Basil D'Oliveira was a great help too. He was tremendous in the guidance and encouragement which he gave to young players. The England bowlers in that Test were Higgs, Geoff Arnold, D'Oliveira, Close, Fred Titmus and Derek Underwood. I had only experienced keeping wicket to two of them – Underwood and Arnold. Later in my Test career I would have wanted to have kept to all of them in practice before the game started, but in those early days I didn't have the experience to know that I should. It was also Arnold's Test debut and the last time we had been on the same side was in the South of England Schools at Cranleigh – home, as I have said, of Peter May, one of the selectors who had given Arnold and me our Test debut. Arnold was one of the great swing bowlers of all time in English conditions. He swung the ball very late, and, especially against the right-handed batsman, could be extremely dangerous. I was to take more catches off him in Test cricket than any other bowler.

It was a long wait for my first ever Test innings. I must have sat with my pads on for over two hours while Ken Barrington was batting. His innings of 109 not out occupied six hours and fifty minutes. It was very dark and gloomy when I did get to the wicket. Mushtaq Mohammad, against whom I had played in Pakistan the previous winter, had me caught at slip by his older brother Hanif – a tentative, nervous shot, playing half back and just nicking it.

Just as I wasn't sure about my first ever catch, so many people might not have seen my first miss, because it was such a thin edge. Asif Iqbal, later to become a colleague at Kent and in World Series Cricket, was the batsman, D'Oliveira the unfortunate bowler. The ball had swung very late and, not spotting it early enough, I had tended to move a little bit to the leg-side. I had my hands in the right place but the ball squeezed straight through them. That's where Godfrey Evans's teaching was so valuable – just pick the ball up as though nothing's happened and get on with the game. On the credit side I was delighted with a diving catch down the leg-side to dismiss Hanif and with another very good catch which was accompanied by a great deal of fortune. Ibadulla, in his second innings, thick-edged a ball from Close down the leg-side. I just managed to sight the ball, going up, and trapped it with my left arm against my chest, with my right hand closing on it. That illustrates the philosophy that you have got to think lucky all the time, especially if things are going wrong.

Ironically, during that Test Kent were playing Yorkshire at Canterbury and my deputy in the county side was Godfrey Evans, who came out of retirement for that one match. Both

counties were challenging for the championship and with Yorkshire's Close and Boycott and Kent's Cowdrey, Underwood and
Knott in the England side there was plenty of interest in the
game's progress. It was a close-fought affair and they announced
the scores regularly at Trent Bridge, which didn't please Close.
His attitude, quite rightly, was: 'Let's concentrate on this Test
match.' During the tea interval we heard about the tremendous
catch on the boundary by Alan Ealham to dismiss Fred Trueman.
Ealham, Kent's substitute that day, was one of the greatest
fielders in the game. He often fielded as 12th man for England
and was unlucky not to have played Test cricket, and particularly
so not to have toured India, because he was such a fine player of
spin bowling.

The third and final Test at the Oval featured that fantastic
century by Asif and his brilliant partnership with Intikhab Alam.
Asif, who came in at number nine, played one of the most
memorable innings you could wish to see. He seemed to be
hitting every ball for four and when we took the new ball he
smashed it everywhere. Eventually, however, he provided me
with my first stumping in Test cricket, off Close.

So I could look back on the 1967 season with a fair degree of
satisfaction – at Test and at county level, because Kent had won
the Gillette Cup in the county's first ever Lord's final. There was a
feeling that I would be in the party to tour the West Indies that
winter – a tour preceded by Close losing the England captaincy,
following incidents as the Yorkshire team were leaving the field
after a game against Warwickshire at Edgbaston. What a way for
Close's captaincy to end – picked by the selectors and then ousted
by the MCC. Thank goodness things have changed since then.
Yet still the odd doubt emerges from Lord's: Mike Denness has
said that he wanted John Snow for the 1974–5 Australian tour but
was told before the selection meeting started that it would not be
possible. You can imagine how relieved the Aussies were.

Having been on the under-25 tour to Pakistan I hadn't felt too
much on strange ground during my first two Tests against them
in England. It was very helpful to know something of their
players in advance and when I left with the England party for the
West Indies tour of 1967–8 I felt I had a similar advantage. For
having been to the Caribbean with the Cavaliers made a
tremendous difference to my first senior tour. I had played

against some of the West Indian team before, experienced the different climate and the wickets. I am sure the more experience you can obtain at an early age improves your feeling for and your approach to the game.

I had felt very ill during the Cavaliers tour, the first time I had been abroad in my life, and it was probably due to the sun. Nor had I forgotten that first flight to the Caribbean. We were fogbound for two days at Heathrow before flying out on a Britannia, first to Newfoundland, where we found ourselves deep in snow, before continuing to Bermuda and on to Jamaica. The consolation for some was that all drinks on the plane were free, but there were times when I thought that we were never going to reach our destination. Fortunately the second flight was more agreeable, but disappointment lay ahead – I was omitted from the team for the first Test at Port of Spain. I had kept in the last two Tests in England and nobody had indicated that there was a chance of my being left out. The morning before the first day of the Test, there was a selection meeting and after it we went into the dressing room to hear the side announced. Colin Cowdrey said, 'Here's the team', and read out the names. I was really disappointed, not necessarily because I wasn't playing but more because no one had said anything to me. I felt somebody should have had a prior word with all those who were not selected. That is all that was necessary and to a young player it would have been so important. When you have had more experience you realize that those sort of tip-offs don't always come your way, but as a youngster you tend to float along, living on the crest of a wave. Since then I have always stressed to captains, when I have been a senior player, that they should try and let people know they are not in the team before it is announced. That should apply at any level in the game. In the past, many Kent players have been heard to say that they had to go and get a scorecard to see what the team was!

It was only after the side for the Test had been revealed that the manager, Les Ames, spoke to me about the selection. He said he was very sorry that I had not been told beforehand and that they had decided to play Jim Parks because they were a bit worried about the batting. I couldn't understand the reason; indeed I thought it was very strange in the light of the batting line-up available – Boycott, Edrich, Barrington, Cowdrey, Graveney,

D'Oliveira. I didn't think they needed Parks's batting, because they had Fred Titmus in the side. The fact that Cowdrey could be a rather defensive-minded captain probably didn't help my cause and the selectors were reasoning that Parks was the player who could get them a hundred if it was needed. Parks had made his Test debut purely as a batsman against Pakistan in 1954 but his first Test as a wicket-keeper/batsman was in the West Indies, at Port of Spain during the 1959–60 tour, when the selectors were looking for the strongest possible batting line-up and he obliged by scoring an unbeaten 101.

Most of us not selected for the opening Test went off for a swim and then out for a drink. We probably all drank a bit more than we should have done. In those days Bacardi and Coke was my favourite and I certainly drank more than I do now. I wasn't drunk, but since then I have always made it a rule to drink very little on the night before a match. Even if you have not been selected, you never know what the fitness of the chosen players may be the next morning and you could be required to play. In fact I had to act as 12th man the following day and was very quickly on the field when Jeff Jones went off with a split web between the fingers. I fielded fine leg and mid-off which would have surprised many of today's professionals who have seen that throwing is no longer one of my strong points – certainly when compared to David Bairstow, who threw so well to run out batsmen in the 1984 one-day internationals against the West Indies. I feel, incidentally, that the 12th-man duty should be shared out so that people not selected have a chance of getting away from the cricket and from the ground if they wish. That is why I felt so sorry for Chris Tavaré on the 1984 winter tour of Pakistan when, because of injury and illness, he was the only person available to do those duties.

That drinking bout in the West Indies made me recall a previous occasion as a youngster when I had had too much to drink. It prevented me taking part in a match. I was selected to play in an important game for the Association of Kent Cricket Clubs under-19 team against Surrey at East Molesey on the Monday. On the Sunday I turned out in a club game for Blackheath at Linden Park. The result was a tie, which was very rare, and we stayed on at the ground for a drink. Blackheath was a very sociable club and as I had been given a lift to the ground I had to wait until my colleagues were ready to leave. When we did get away it was very late and like everyone else I had had a fair share of drink. Everyone was hungry and one of our party knocked up a Chinese restaurant in Tunbridge Wells. It was closed but the proprietor accepted the offer of a generous sum of money to open up and serve us a meal. I had just started to eat when I felt I was going to be sick and rushed out to the toilet. I felt very ill and when I got up the next morning I was sick every time I stood. So my mother had to ring George Fowler, who was in charge of the AKCC side, and say that I was ill and would not be able to play. (How much I and many Kent players owe Mr Fowler and George Pope, who ran Kent schools, for their early guidance and encouragement!) I spent the day lying on a settee and realized that if I was going to play cricket professionally this kind of behaviour could not be repeated. It was a lesson learned very early. I didn't stop drinking, but I never drank that quantity again.

Certainly I didn't repeat my drinking when I was left out of the second Test at Kingston and the third at Bridgetown. Parks had kept exceptionally well in the three Tests but he couldn't get a score together. Yet he was a marvellous player of spin bowling and much of that series saw us opposed to spinners like Lance Gibbs, Sobers, Willie Rodriguez, David Holford and Inshan Ali. Maybe it was because Gibbs was such a force for the West Indies that I found myself, as an off-spinner, doing a lot of bowling in the nets while I was out of the side. Sometimes it seemed that it was always Boycott at the other end, but I enjoyed it because it brought back memories of my early bowling days. Before the third Test in Barbados I was told that Parks was having a fitness test on the morning of the match. The impression was given that I might play. Cowdrey, however, seemed keen for Parks to play and talked him into it. Unfortunately he was dismissed for a duck, first ball, leg before to Lance Gibbs. I used to operate his cine-camera for him during those early Tests but on this occasion I hadn't even reached the television tower before he was returning to the pavilion.

I was recalled for the fourth Test at Trinidad in the hope that my batting would come off. Ironically, batting was needed in those last two Tests. During that series Cowdrey's consistency as a batsman was superb and at Trinidad in the second innings he played better than I had ever seen him. It was a very difficult wicket, with the ball turning appreciably, but he hit the spinners everywhere. I never saw him play too many innings of that calibre, chasing runs against spin bowlers. Cowdrey scored his 71 in seventy-six minutes during a match-winning stand of 118 with Boycott. When Cowdrey was out Boycott steered us home with three minutes to spare, finishing unbeaten on 80. Cowdrey was a great accumulator of runs. Generally he limited himself to certain shots, looking for the ball on his legs and working it from in front of square to fine leg for the ones and twos. He also favoured running the ball down through the gully area, allowing the ball to run off the face of the bat. He loved playing the wrist-spinner, employing the cover drive so well against them, particularly the leg-spinner. He would challenge himself to pierce the gaps in the covers by opening or closing the face of the bat to change the direction of the ball. He seemed to hit it just hard enough for it to reach the boundary, almost as though he were teasing the fielders in the covers. My first ever Test partnership with Cowdrey was in that fourth Test. When I joined him we were 260 for 5, pursuing a West Indies' first innings of 526 for 7 declared. We added 113 runs at almost three an over and of course I was delighted to reach my first Test half-century.

Cowdrey was very good to the young player. People criticized him for analysing the technique of the game but, like him, I found it very interesting. Although it was a professional contest out in the middle he got a lot of fun from his part in it. He loved batting and working out different theories. People have suggested he might have been a better player if he had not been analytical but I cannot believe he would have been any better. It is terribly important to analyse. Cowdrey was a great help to me in those very early days in how to play Sobers when the ball was swinging. It was causing me plenty of trouble but Cowdrey made me look to push forward, on delivery, and play down the line of the stumps. As the ball swung in, the bat was in position to protect the wicket. If it didn't swing but went straight on you tried to let it go. Your instinct was to move your feet right across the wicket to Sobers and if he made one swing back in you could be leg before. It seemed as if he was always bowling towards second slip but he had this great ability to make the ball dip in late. If it hit you on the pads you were generally trapped in front of the wicket. Cowdrey would watch a young player, spot the problems and ask how he could help to solve them. He made you feel you could do it. He loved to watch batsmen, assessing their strengths and weaknesses. He just liked to see people batting, from the classical style to the completely unorthodox player, who always interested him. He was also always seeking to improve his own game. If he turned out in benefit matches he would use his innings to work on some new idea. Whenever or wherever he played he seemed to enjoy batting.

I always felt he might have enjoyed it even more if he hadn't the worries of captaincy. The role brings added responsibility and difficult decisions. A captain needs to be consistent, cool and quick-witted under pressure, patient and have great understanding of the individual players' personalities. It can cause tremendous pressure – who to drop, where to bat people, when to bowl different players. Cowdrey's greatest qualities as a captain were his ability to use defensive tactics, especially in the bowling of Derek Underwood, and he was a master of public relations in dealing with administrators and the media. I didn't think captaincy suited Cowdrey, but whatever reservations I had about that, as a batsman he was terrific.

It seems strange to recall now, with West Indies pacemen dominating the Test scene, that on that 1967–8 tour we had a genuine trio of fast bowlers in John Snow, David Brown and Jeff Jones who were better than any strike bowlers the opposition could produce. Neither Wes Hall nor Charlie Griffith was fully fit, taking nine and ten wickets respectively in the series. Brown and Jones took fourteen apiece while Snow, who bowled brilliantly, bagged twenty-seven victims at a cost of 19.66 each. He beat the bat consistently on grassless wickets. He always swung the ball late and sometimes so late that it was swinging just before it pitched, giving the impression that it was seaming.

That final Test in Georgetown, Guyana, provided me with one of my best cricket memories. A youngster, playing in only my fourth Test, I was able to help England draw a match which enabled us to win the series. Just picture the scene – the opposition want just one more wicket to win a Test and draw the series; they fail to get it and you are one of the batsmen responsible. How many opportunities do you get in a cricket career to have that very satisfying experience? We had to bat all day to save the match and were 46 for 5 when I joined Cowdrey at the wicket –

before lunch! Our partnership lasted until Cowdrey's dismissal seventy minutes from the close and then the batsmen to come were Snow, Tony Lock, the hero of the first innings with a best-ever score of 89, Pat Pocock and Jeff Jones. The ball was turning and bouncing but we reached the last over with our number eleven, the Welshman Jones, at the wicket to face Gibbs. When Jones came in I said to him, 'Good luck! If we can stick this out there'll be a welcome in the hillsides for you tonight.' I reckoned there would still be time for another over and when Jones arrived in the middle we agreed that we wouldn't change ends because it would mean him facing Sobers's chinamen and googlies. The fifth ball of the over hit Jones in the chest as he played forward extraordinarily low and we could have run a leg-bye, but we turned it down because we thought that there would be another over. After Gibbs had bowled the sixth ball I was about to mark my crease and prepare to combat Sobers when umpire Kippins said, 'That's time.' I was so relieved that the match was over and delighted that the series was won.

The tension didn't end there, however, because as we left the field the crowd reacted badly, disappointed that their favourites had not managed to level the series. There were unpleasant scenes when we were leaving the ground and Lock was struck on the head by a stone as we emerged from the dressing rooms to be driven away in taxis.

There had been crowd trouble earlier in the tour, during the second Test in Jamaica. Spectators rioted after Basil Butcher had been given out, brilliantly caught down the leg-side by Parks, and tear gas had to be used to control them.

One way or another it had been a never-to-be-forgotten tour, which provided me with my first taste of highly pressurized Test cricket.

# *Four*

# Keeping Heyday

Having kept wicket to Derek Underwood at international and county level for twenty years, I have enjoyed a privileged view of most of his notable triumphs, and none was more opportune than that 7 for 50 on a wet wicket at the Oval in 1968 which enabled us to square the series against Australia. It did not prevent the Aussies from retaining the Ashes but what a dramatic finish to that final Test, when the crowd gladly helped ground staff mop up the surface water after a thunderstorm and torrential rain had threatened to end the game. Instead it restarted and Underwood bowled Australia to defeat.

What really surprises me is that youngsters who must have watched Underwood for many years on television have not copied his style of bowling. He is one of the all-time cricketing greats and I would have expected that young cricketers would try and copy him. His great assets are his run-up, delivery and follow-through – they are perfect. He has a rhythmical and economical approach to the wicket, and he makes full use of his body in delivery, while obtaining maximum height in his action, with a perfect follow-through. In fact if you read the MCC coaching book you will find he has the classic method of bowling. It has provided him with accuracy of length and line and enabled him to look after his body throughout his professional career. He has hardly ever missed a match. I remember once after he had been bowling at Bournemouth non-stop through an innings, Hampshire's Nigel Cowley came into the dressing room and said, 'I wish I had your legs.' The wonderful thing about him, which goes unnoticed, is his supreme cricket fitness. He is one of the old school who always believes that to get fit for bowling you bowl and bowl, whether in the middle or in the nets, although he much prefers the middle. As the years have gone by he has been noticed occasionally running round the outfield for training and has taken up a little exercising, something which until a few years ago was unheard of as far as he was concerned.

He is a world-class bowler on any type of wicket and the best bowler of all on a really turning wicket, whether wet or dusty. Funnily enough it was not until 1984 that many of his new colleagues in the Kent team had ever seen him bowl on a rain-affected pitch. It was at Canterbury against Hampshire, when the water had got under the covers, and Underwood was in his element. The youngsters stared in disbelief as the ball turned and lifted and he was virtually unplayable. Terry Alderman, the Australian Test bowler, who was with Kent for the season, stood at slip and reckoned that for the batsman it was as dangerous as facing Dennis Lillee. Underwood's competitive attitude has been of immense value to his bowling and it has shone through in his batting. He has only once in his career failed as a night-watchman to get through to the end of the day's play – what an extra-ordinary record. He was as delighted to return to his happiest hunting ground at Hastings to score his maiden first-class century in the 1984 season as he was when he registered his best bowling return there twenty years earlier. That century, on a very bad wicket, was remarkable because he completely dominated the innings against an attack which included a world-class bowler like Garth Le Roux. Underwood gave only one chance, to skipper John Barclay at second slip when he had scored 96.

How lucky I have been to have kept wicket from the age of fourteen, watching a true master learn his trade and practise it in a way that has never been equalled. I only hope that when I coach in the future I can copy the action!

Making his first visit to England in the summer of 1968 was John Gleeson, the Australian spinner, who was a bowler I always studied closely. At Brisbane during the 1970–1 tour, I went above the sightscreen to look at him bowling for a long spell. He could bowl a leg-break, giving the appearance that it was an off-break, and vice versa. Gleeson held the ball between thumb and second finger, which was bent, while his forefinger jutted out straight, the top part not touching the ball. The second finger was the spinning agent, laid along the seam, and was flipped out powerfully from its bent position on delivery as he undercut the ball, making his leg break look like an off break. The palm of his hand was towards the batsman. He bowled two types of ball, which came in to the right hander. For his off break the protruding finger was brought down on the seam just before delivery and the wrist turned clockwise. His second type of ball was bowled more like a googly, with the back of the hand facing the batsman. The ball was flicked out over the top of his hand with his powerful second finger but because his wrist was facing a different way the ball turned in the opposite direction. I reckoned the best way of trying to spot what he was doing was to bowl as he bowled and I learned with some success with a tennis ball over a short distance, but nowhere near as well over twenty-two yards with a cricket ball. My Gleeson-type delivery, however, did yield me the scalps of two big names – Geoff Boycott in the nets at Trent Bridge in 1969, and Brian Luckhurst in the Melbourne indoor school during the 1970–1 tour, both clean bowled. Boycott was probably as amazed as me. Surprisingly, Bill Lawry, the Australian captain, rarely used Gleeson as an attacking bowler. When he was brought on, the fielders were generally back and he was bowled in a defensive capacity. I felt he would have been a great attacking bowler, with fielders close to the wicket on each side, for bat-and-pad catches.

Lawry was one of the nicest people you could wish to meet but on the field he was fiercely competitive. I have seen him going up to appeal for a leg-before decision when he has been fielding at square leg, and when he was batting he would do anything to avoid being given out, rubbing himself anywhere if there was an appeal for a catch at the wicket. At Melbourne in 1970–1, when there was nothing in the Test, Lawry suddenly declared with Rodney Marsh in the 90s, an incredible decision because Marsh would have been the first Australian wicket-keeper to have scored a century in a Test match.

It was in the second Test at Lord's in 1968 that I held one of my best-ever catches – and Lawry was the victim. He got an inside edge off David Brown, bowling with the new ball, and I dived wide to my right and managed to catch it, my hand skidding along the ground.

My experience in the first Test at Old Trafford had not been too happy because in England's second innings I played one of my most disappointing knocks. I have always enjoyed batting under pressure and we really were up against it when I went in. Anybody who bats from number six to nine should be trained for pressure. I played a dreadful shot against Alan Connolly, attempting to pull a ball which was not a short-pitched delivery, and was out leg before.

The tour to South Africa in the winter of 1968–9, which would have been my first there, was called off when the D'Oliveira affair blew up. It seems strange that D'Oliveira didn't play throughout that series against Australia, which would have made him a fairly certain choice for the touring party. Instead, having scored 87 in the second innings of the first Test, easily the top England score of the match – and on a bad wicket – he was left out for the next three Tests. He was restored to the side for the final Test and made 158, only to be omitted from the tour. Then Tom Cartwright dropped out of the party and D'Oliveira, principally a batsman, was chosen to replace a man selected principally as a bowler. I was just on my way to the airport to leave for a holiday in Majorca when the news came through that the South African tour had been abandoned.

We spent that winter instead in Pakistan, where my chance of a first Test century was foiled by riots in Karachi in the third Test. I was 96 not out and had been beaten all ends up by a googly from Mushtaq Mohammad, the ball passing over the top of the stumps, beating the wicket-keeper Wasim Bari too and going for a bye. I could easily have been out to that delivery and was just preparing to face the next ball when David Brown, my partner, called, 'Come on, let's get off.' We raced back to the pavilion, hotly pursued by the fielders and umpires, reaching the safety of the dressing room without any incident. Then the rioters vented their fury on the wicket, which they began to dig up. We had been warned that there was serious unrest among Pakistan's students and that it would possibly lead them to the cricket ground. Yet when they arrived I had not noticed them because I was concentrating so hard on the match.

I have never worried about hundreds. My theory has always been that it was nice to get 90. There were never any nervous nineties for me – there is not much difference between scoring 98 and 102 unless you lose the match by four runs. During my career I have seen matches ruined by the determination to allow a player to reach his century. In 1981 at the Oval the Australians batted on for Dirk Welham to reach his 100. He was pushing for singles and struggling to find the gaps; we were very happy about it because we didn't want to have to bat for an hour or so that evening. Ian Botham told him, 'Whatever you do, don't throw it away now', and the batsman was obviously under tremendous pressure. The story emerged about Botham being a wonderful sportsman but it could have been a great tactical move on his part to try and keep the Aussies at the crease and maintain their slow progress. Certainly that was the strategy of Mike Brearley, the England skipper. I felt that if we had batted that evening and lost a couple of wickets Australia should have won the match. In a championship match at Leeds, Bill Athey, now with Gloucestershire but then a Yorkshire player, was told to play for his century. He managed it, but Yorkshire got only three batting points against us and it should have been four. It was unbelievable; they should easily have reached 300 in their 100 overs. All that is changing – in my early days people generally played for their century, but it is going out of the game now. Rightly so, because if you bat with that attitude you could be responsible for altering the pattern of the whole game.

The summer of 1969, when Ray Illingworth took over the England captaincy after Colin Cowdrey had torn an Achilles' tendon, saw me reach my peak as a wicket-keeper. It came during the third Test against the West Indies and continued during the three matches against New Zealand. My seven best years as a wicket-keeper were between 1966 and 1972. In 1969 I was named Man of the Series against the West Indies and Wisden honoured me as one of their five Cricketers of the Year. Then just before the final Test in Australia on the 1970–1 tour, Bill O'Reilly, the former Aussie Test cricketer, wrote the most favourable article I have ever read about myself.

Since that time the biggest disappointment in my career was that I could never again keep wicket so well. Perhaps there was a great advantage in reaching my wicket-keeping peak as young as

I did, but there has been tremendous frustration at not being able to return to that standard. I did try hard, but never made it. After 1972 I maintained a standard which kept me in the Test side and occasionally had very good periods behind the stumps. My determination and mental attitude were still good but there were slight cracks appearing in my technique. My body, not really suited to keeping wicket, was beginning to hinder my technique.

One of the interesting reasons why we beat the West Indies in that 1969 series was that Barry Knight seemed to get the measure of Gary Sobers. Illingworth set up the ploy which involved Knight bowling a very full length, just outside the off stump, to Sobers, which caused him problems. He twice had him caught by Phil Sharpe at slip as he edged the ball. Then Knight's dismissal of Sobers in the third Test at Headingley was vital. Sobers had obviously planned to get right across to safeguard the edges to slip and dragged the ball on to his wicket with an inside edge from well outside off stump. It was just typical of Illingworth's shrewd ability as a captain and he was really seen at his very best in that third Test, one of his three greatest Tests. The West Indies should have won comfortably but Illingworth inspired a magnificent performance in the field and he and Derek Underwood bowled brilliantly.

So the winter of 1969–70 found me coaching and playing in Tasmania at a stage when I felt I was at my wicket-keeping peak. Rohan Kanhai and I were there together, following in the footsteps of Australian Test bowler Neil Hawke, who subsequently became very seriously ill. He became a Christian while he was ill, I'm told, and made a miraculous recovery. Jack Hampshire and David Evans (former Glamorgan wicket-keeper and now a Test umpire) were also out in Tasmania; Jack Simmons, the Lancashire all-rounder, had many winters on the island; and former Leicestershire player Brian Davison has been there. One of the points I emphasized during my stay was that they should do everything possible to get into the Sheffield Shield. They had some very talented players, but as in other sports it is impossible to get to the top level if you are not playing at that standard. It has been very satisfying to see that they have managed to get into the top competitions and have done well.

In 1970, with the South African tour to this country cancelled, England met the Rest of the World in a series which was much closer than the 4–1 margin in their favour suggested. It could easily have been 2–2 had we won the Headingley match. It was a very tight finish and if we had got Barry Richards out, as we thought we had, there was only Lance Gibbs to come – and the new ball was due. It was a very competitive series, playing against fantastic opposition. What a wonderful batting line up it was – Barry Richards, Eddie Barlow, Rohan Kanhai, Graeme Pollock, Clive Lloyd, Gary Sobers, Mushtaq Mohammad, Farokh Engineer, Mike Procter.

The year 1970 was a memorable one for Kent – we won the county championship for the first time since 1913. It was an unusual county season for me, batting once at number three and for the rest of the campaign anywhere between numbers six and ten. Twice I didn't get in when batting at number ten and yet I had averaged 30 in the five Tests against the Rest of the World, batting at number seven.

That was the start of Kent's glory years of the seventies. The team Mike Denness led at Kent must have been one of the best county sides ever; looking back now it is hard to believe that such a powerful unit could exist. I count myself extremely lucky to have been part of it. In one-day cricket particularly we were exceptionally difficult to beat. Of course it is impossible to win all the time, but we always felt that in limited-overs cricket the opposition would really have to play very well and have everything going their way to defeat us.

The reason for our pre-eminence lay in the quantity and quality of our all-rounders. Asif Iqbal, John Shepherd, Bernard Julien and Bob Woolmer were all supremely good. Asif, Shepherd and Julien all opened the bowling for their countries while Woolmer played for England as a bowler in one-day internationals. In addition, they were all very fine batsmen. Had Shepherd not been hit on the head and injured by David Brown on England's tour to the West Indies in 1967–8 I am certain he would have opened the batting for them in the next Test. Asif, of course, was one of the world's most attractive stroke players, Woolmer became the leading batsman in the England side in 1977, and Julien had enormous potential in that department.

There were unsung members of the side too. Richard Hills was a reliable all-rounder in the squad. A swing bowler who had a fair bit of zip, he was also adept at chasing runs in the lower order.

Alan Ealham was a very exciting batsman. You always knew something was going to happen. He was a brilliant fielder, known as 'Buckets' because of his catching, and he earned a reputation as one of the most spectacular fielders in the country. Indeed, the Kent team generally were magnificent in the field.

Looking at the side written down on paper now it is remarkable to think that such a wonderful team could be chosen from this squad: Cowdrey, Denness, Luckhurst, Asif, Ealham, Shepherd, Julien, Knott, Woolmer, Johnson, Underwood, Hills, Graham, Dye, Jarvis.

Inevitably, all great sides break up. Some players got older, and Kent county did not really help themselves; I was amazed when Hills wasn't retained and staggered when they released Julien – here was a player of high international class and they were letting him go. It was also a great mistake to let Mike Denness go to Essex.

If only Kent had encouraged Woolmer's talent by making him captain at some stage. What a player he was before back injury forced him to retire from the first-class game in 1984. He and I have had some great times together, whether it's been coaching, playing or sightseeing in the various countries we have visited. Recently I helped him with the production of a coaching video, *Let's Play Cricket*, with a narrative by Christopher Martin-Jenkins, the commentator.

In 1981 Woolmer had been given a trial run as Kent captain. He had a very good cricket brain and tremendous enthusiasm for the game. He was popular with the players, was a very good coach and, because of his own attitude towards and understanding of difficult personalities, he got the best out of his men, who knew he could help their cricket no matter what their department. He captained Kent four times during the 1981 season and we won three of the games, only being denied a fourth victory when rain intervened with their last pair at the crease. Despite those successes, Woolmer never led Kent again.

In 1982 the county decided that if Asif were absent the side would be led by Chris Tavaré or Chris Cowdrey. Tavaré, appointed Kent captain in 1983, is a completely different player according to the type of match he is engaged in. In one-day cricket he can be one of the most dangerous players in the country, hitting the ball extremely powerfully. In county cricket, in run chases, he can employ the same methods and, in fact, can rarely be blamed for slow scoring. At Test level, however, he can be a very different batsman, playing for time and letting the runs come. He obviously enjoys defending as well as attacking and I am sure he has nearly always been encouraged to play defensively in Tests, although he has proved that he can play shots as well at that level.

Despite his quiet voice, Tavaré has a very strong character, putting forward his thoughts firmly but pleasantly. He is flexible, though, and if you want to chat to him and try to persuade him, he will listen. He believes in discipline and applies it cleverly, making his feelings known, but with the knack of stopping the development of any situation that could be getting out of control. During his captaincy, for example, he made it perfectly clear that he wanted his players fit in the morning before the day's play and that he was not going to tolerate late nights or heavy drinking. He is one of the few players in the game to wear a gum shield and that makes it very difficult to hear his call when batting, so players sometimes kid him about his muffled calling. As a captain, Tavaré's calm character really shone through. He was marvellous under pressure, pulling us through many tense one-day games when the odds were stacked against us, and it was sad to see him lose the job at the end of 1984.

While wishing Chris Cowdrey every success as captain, I feel a little sorry for him because he has had to take a lot of pressure. Kent were not talented enough to be rated in the top four counties in 1983 and 1984, yet they did superbly well under Tavaré's leadership and reached two NatWest Trophy finals. They are improving all the time with experience and it seems as if Cowdrey will be expected to lead them to victory in at least one competition. That will not be easy with such fine opponents as Middlesex, Nottinghamshire, Somerset and Essex, but if the captaincy inspires Cowdrey to stay fit and become an England standard bowler, that could be a very vital factor for Kent. It could also secure him a regular England place. His excellent batting gained him a Test place and he is one of the finest all-round fielders you could wish to see. He is a marvellous entertainer and, like Tavaré, a very likeable personality.

# *Five*

# Captain Supreme

The best captain I ever played under was Ray Illingworth. It was Illingworth who led the England team in Australia during the 1970–1 series when we won back the Ashes. He was a tremendous captain, always getting the best out of his players. He gave me the feeling that we could win under his leadership in any situation. He was always prepared to fight on, convinced that you had to give everything until the game was won or lost. He was a very decisive person. He would ask people for their opinions but you always knew that he would make a positive decision in the end. He knew the game inside out and whatever might go wrong, you thought that he could make it right. You could be losing a game but he could still get the best out of everybody and transform it, as the opposition might start to panic or play badly.

The second of Illingworth's three greatest Tests as captain was the fifth Test at Sydney. Our fast bowlers had done very well on the tour; suddenly we were without John Snow on the last day because he had damaged a finger very badly when crashing into the perimeter fence while fielding the previous day. I reckoned at that point that Australia were favourites to win the match. Illingworth, contrary to most people's expectations, didn't bowl his pacemen; he bowled himself with Derek Underwood. Rod

Marsh was dismissed by Underwood; Illingworth got rid of Greg Chappell; then Basil D'Oliveira snatched two wickets with successive balls, and we won by 62 runs.

Illingworth's performances with bat and ball for his country, especially after he became captain, were frequently exceptional. He was an excellent and courageous catcher in front of the wicket on the off-side, and he confirmed his ability as a leader when he moved to Leicestershire and took over the captaincy. When he returned to Yorkshire as manager I felt he was the one person who would sort out their problems. What happened during his spell in that role, which ended with his departure during the winter of 1983–4, I cannot imagine. If there was any problem in the game of cricket I would have backed 'Illy' to find the solution. Certainly during that 1970–1 tour he had got the best out of Geoff Boycott, who played superbly in the sixth Test at Adelaide for his 119 not out. We were looking to declare and Boycott, who had a brilliant tour, obviously carried out Illingworth's instructions to score his runs quickly. On another occasion, also at Adelaide, but earlier in the tour in a State match, Boycott had been instructed by the skipper to get himself out as soon as possible, having batted throughout the previous day. Boycott was not very happy but he complied with the order, getting caught behind the wicket down the leg-side for 173. What a waste it is to cricket that Illingworth is not still in the game as an administrator. At one stage he must have been the number-one choice to be cricket's supremo of the future.

There was an amusing example of Illingworth's ingenuity off the field during the fifth Test at Sydney. Bob Taylor, who was 12th man, had gone out to sunbathe at the back of the pavilion while we were batting, and when he didn't return Illingworth became concerned about who would take out the drinks. It was agreed that I should deputize, being the only one of Bob's height and colouring, but something had to be done about my hair. Bob was only grey in the front then, so the lads powdered my hair and sent me out with the tray of drinks. Not many people realized it was me until I reached the middle, when Ian Chappell, the Aussies' skipper, spotted who I was. He wasn't very pleased. As I had not yet batted he didn't think I should be out there, sampling the atmosphere in the middle – and he said so. Occasionally with Ian you could not be quite sure whether he was serious or not, but I don't think he was joking then. Our lads thought it was very amusing and just after I returned to the dressing room Bob rushed back in a panic, having dozed off while he lay sunbathing.

It was later on that tour, when we had moved on to New Zealand, that Bob made his Test debut – in the first Test at Christchurch. I was obviously delighted for him but very upset about the decision and the way in which it was handled. Some days earlier I had heard rumours through one or two of the senior players that there were thoughts of leaving me out and playing Bob as a reward for his undoubted loyalty on the tour. I didn't think that was right, because in Test cricket you should always select your best side at that time. A player's chance should always come through either injury or loss of form. In conversation with Illingworth I said that I had heard the rumours and wanted to make it clear that I did not agree with the policy. He agreed with me that the best team should always be chosen. After the selectors' meeting I was on my way to a restaurant for a meal with a group of players, including Bob Taylor, when I ran into Illingworth. He told me that the selectors had decided to reward Bob by giving him a game in the Test. I was amazed that Illingworth should have changed his mind or have had it changed for him. I didn't query it but said that I was on my way to have a meal with Bob and would he like me to tell him. Illingworth agreed and I was delighted to have the chance to give Bob his good news. Bob Willis, who was left out of the match for a similar reason, was rooming with me, so there were two very disappointed players together.

Because things had gone so well in Australia it had been decided that everyone should play a Test. There were various stories in the newspapers – one suggested that Illingworth felt that the other players had deserved a Test chance; another expressed the view that I had agreed to stand down in order to give Bob Taylor a game. The latter idea was certainly not correct, because my view was that at Test level the people in form should keep playing. A player's career can change dramatically and if he misses out when he is playing well he could return to the side and find himself struggling for form. It was a very rare occasion when I had found Illingworth to be inconsistent, but it is possible that he had been outvoted by the other selectors – David Clark, a former Kent chairman, who was the tour manager, Colin Cowdrey and John Edrich. With 12th-man duties I did not see much of the cricket but from what I did manage to see Bob unfortunately did not perform at his best on a turning wicket. Apart from the wonderful memory of becoming an England player, his first Test was probably not one he would want to remember. It had been made clear to me that I would return for the second Test at Auckland. There I scored 101, my first Test century, and 96, prompting Derek Underwood to remark jokingly, 'They should leave you out more often if that's the way you come back.'

The 1970–1 tour was my first with Taylor, who, when I first started playing, was not nationally thought of as a potential England wicket-keeper. As I neared Test selection the wicket-keepers I felt that I needed to get in front of were Jimmy Binks, John Murray and Jim Parks. Of those on the way up the more prominent two seemed to be Eifion Jones, of Glamorgan, and Roger Tolchard, who was enjoying great success under the captaincy of Tony Lock at Leicestershire. In those early days Tolchard showed great promise with his wicket-keeping and, of course, always looked a fine batsman. Jones seemed certain in my view to go on tour for England. He was a very fine all-round 'keeper, with a lot of batting talent, and he must have been disappointed that he was not chosen for the 1970–1 Australian tour. Somebody with Jones's ability as a wicket-keeper and batsman should have had top honours in front of him, yet not only has he never played for England but he has never been involved in a representative game.

There was a strange revelation at Trent Bridge in 1976 when I reported for England duty with a broken finger. Tolchard, who had not fulfilled his early promise as a 'keeper, was called up to stand by. When we were talking about my fitness to play, Alec Bedser said, 'If we had thought there was any real doubt we would have asked Bob Taylor.' Charlie Elliott, then a selector, added, 'We chose Roger because we thought you might be more worried about him embarrassing you with his batting, and that might persuade you to play.' Charlie was a great motivator throughout my Test career and I am sure said this only to encourage me to play. The biggest boost I received as a younger wicket-keeper was when Brian Close and Ray Illingworth, both Yorkshiremen, picked me in their England sides in preference to

Jimmy Binks. Binks always won my highest admiration as a wicket-keeper. He had the best technique I ever saw standing up to the wicket, where I can't remember seeing him missing a ball in matches I played against him.

Taylor and I have had very different careers. He seems to have got better and better as he has got older, whereas my early years were my best. As I have grown older, so it has been more difficult to maintain a high standard. But even if technique is lacking, mental attitude can get you through. You accept that you can no longer do some of the things you used to do, but as long as you keep trying your weaknesses may not be exposed. So you have to back your strong points, and the main thing is not to allow your confidence to slip. It is all down to body types. Bob, for example, has got better and stayed very supple and strong. In Adelaide in 1970–1 when we did stretching exercises it was obvious that there was a massive difference in our mobility. If you ever want proof of his strength and mobility you should see him perform his Cossack dance. I have always rated him one of the fittest crick-eters in the game. I think the best two years he had were in 1978, the season in which I didn't play at all, and 1982, the first year of my three-year ban for playing in the South African tour.

I have often been conscious of the situation between Bob and myself. We are different personalities but we have always been friends and there was never any animosity between us (though, for a period of ten years or more, we have been in direct competition for a Test place). Whenever Taylor said, 'Good luck' or 'Well done' it was always genuine. Obviously he always wanted to play and it was a great relief to me that he established himself after I had joined World Series Cricket. I just don't know how I would have felt at the end of my career if I had managed to keep him out of the England side, with no chance to reveal his talent at the top level. I have often thought it would have been interesting to compare both of us at our peak, the Knott of, say, 1969, as a twenty-three-year-old, with the Taylor of around 1978, a thirty-seven-year-old. When it came to analysing our game, practising and training, we were in our element and I can recall a very long discussion we had with Rodney Marsh about wicket-keeping techniques. Bob was extremely talented and I always felt sorry that only one of us could play. Fortunately it was never my decision – that is what selectors are for. Perhaps it was because of my batting, but I never felt that I was going to lose my Test place. Only early in the West Indies in 1973, when I wasn't playing very well as a batsman or wicket-keeper, did I feel guilty about keeping someone else out. There could have been a question-mark over my Test place and I discussed my form with Geoff Boycott, one of the senior players. His advice was not to worry about it and he virtually told me: never seek to drop yourself – wait for someone else to do that.

Having made my international debut against Pakistan it was appropriate that I registered my first Test century in England against them in 1971. It was in the first Test at Edgbaston, with the weather pattern typical of that ground. They batted for two days in the sunshine and took our attack apart, with Zaheer Abbas making his highest-ever score of 274. When we batted it was a murky day, with the ball nipping off the wicket. Imran Khan was making his Test debut but it was Asif Masood who did the damage as England were reduced to 127 for 5 by the time I reached the crease. In those days I really used to have a go at the spinners and Intikhab kept them on, hoping that I would get myself out. Runs came quickly for me and I had some good fortune. For when Masood was restored to the attack I struck him for four boundaries and he was removed, which was probably a mistake. The third Test at Headingley was also the third of the 'Illingworth greats'. He led us to a superb victory when we could well have lost, applying so much pressure that we were able to bowl them out. That was the match in which Wasim Bari took eight catches, most of them brilliant, and when I walked round the ground a spectator shouted, 'That's the way to keep wicket.' At his peak Bari was the most consistent all-round wicket-keeper in the game. His mental attitude was perfect.

There was no MCC tour in the winter of 1971–2 and I declined the opportunity to go to Australia with the Rest of the World. After two winters Down Under, coaching in Tasmania in 1969–70 and touring Australia and New Zealand in 1970–1, I really felt the need for a rest. The authorities at Lord's were not worried about my decision. Indeed they were keen for me not to go because they were concerned that if I made the trip I might not want to be involved in the following winter's tour with MCC to India and Pakistan. It was the vogue in those days for some of the senior players to opt out of that trip. It was on that Rest of the World tour that Tony Greig, who could only just have missed selection for Australia in 1970–1, proved what a great player he was and returned to the England side in 1972. I settled down during the winter to write my first book and hoped to take a job coaching soccer in schools. I had been to the labour exchange, where the man who interviewed me said that I should have to sign on the dole. I mentioned to him that I was writing a book, on which I put in a lot of work, but he said that was not relevant. So I signed on, but meanwhile the coaching job had fallen through and nothing similar was forthcoming. Then suddenly a story appeared in a Sunday newspaper about me being on the dole, referring to the fact that I was writing a book. I was advised by my then agent to pay back the dole money that I had received. The affair stayed with me for a few years because even in Australia, during the 1974–5 tour, some of the Aussie fans made remarks about the dole.

The summer of 1972 provided English cricket fans with their first view of Dennis Lillee. We retained the Ashes but Lillee took the honours for the Aussies with a new record for an Australian bowler of thirty-one wickets in a series in England. We had always appreciated that Lillee was going to be a great bowler. He could swing and seam the ball away from the right-hander, which is vital at the top level; he was genuinely quick, young and fit – he had everything. The Aussies were delighted to win the final Test to draw the series. We could have won it but for an unfortunate injury to Illingworth, who sprained his ankle an hour before the close on the fourth day. Had he been there for the final day, his captaincy would have sustained the pressure. The wicket was taking spin too and he was a great bowler in a tight situation. It was a strange decision by Australia to leave Ian Redpath out of their squad for that series. He was a very good player, with an admirable technique against pace bowling, a fine competitor, and had done very well against us in the 1970–1 series. In fact, Redpath was over here that summer and was living in Swanley, where we were neighbours.

That season I struggled with the bat in the early stages, and not having played throughout the winter, took the chance of a game with the Kent second eleven, to have some batting practice. The game was at Chiswick, on a bad wicket, against a Middlesex side that included some names later to become well known – Norman

Featherstone, Harry Latchman, Mike Selvey, John Emburey and Larry Gomes, who played so well over here for the West Indies in 1984. It was appropriately at Maidstone Week – Mote Park is my favourite Kent ground – that I came good with the bat again, scoring a century in each innings against Surrey.

In neither innings at Mote Park did I bat wearing a cap, which was my usual custom, and in the first innings I dropped another of my regular habits – touching the bails on arrival at the crease. It wasn't superstition, as many people thought – it was merely my way of saying to myself, 'You're out in the middle now,' to switch on the concentration. Often a player has sat in the dressing room, waiting to bat, in a completely different world, and he needs to do something to alert himself to the job in hand. Viv Richards bangs his bat handle; Chris Tavaré takes a little walk away from the crease; other batsmen bang their bats just behind the return crease. It all helps to summon up the utmost concentration. When I went out to bat against Surrey in that first innings, Arnold Long put his hands over the top of the bails. I said, 'Don't worry about it, Arnie, I've got to stop doing that,' and I did.

The 1972 season was the beginning of a new era for Kent, particularly in the one-day competitions. We had won the Gillette Cup in 1967 but in 1972 we won the John Player League, the first of eight limited-overs trophies we lifted in seven seasons. Mike Denness had taken over the Kent captaincy that summer from Colin Cowdrey, who had never seemed very enthusiastic about the one-day game. But Denness was keen, and he developed into the best leader I played under in limited-overs cricket.

The 1972–3 tour to India and Pakistan provided examples of players refusing to join overseas tours. Illingworth declined the trip and it was a great shame. If he had gone we would have been a much better side and his experience as a top all-rounder and his brilliant leadership would have altered the pattern of the series. Instead of losing it 2–1, I am sure we would have won it. Apart from Illingworth, John Snow, Geoff Boycott and John Edrich all missed the tour and there seemed little pressure put on them to change their minds. Basil D'Oliveira was another absentee, yet both his batting and his bowling, off-spin as well as medium pace, could have been so useful.

The tour itself started well when we won the first Test by six wickets at Delhi. It staggered me though that we were playing

Test cricket on Christmas Day – that was the final day. It just didn't seem right. Now that I am a Christian, the personal decision as to whether I should play would be very awkward.

The series in India and subsequently in Pakistan brought mixed fortune for me personally – illness, brushes with the tour manager and disappointment with my batting. During the first Test I remember feeling ill as I sat with my pads on while Tony Lewis, who had taken over the captaincy, and Tony Greig featured in the match-winning partnership. I felt so bad that I wondered whether or not I should mention it to anyone. I didn't and in the end my services were not required.

In the second Test at Calcutta there was an unusual incident when in the Indian's second innings the ball went out of shape and became soft very early on. Someone brought out a box of alternative balls and somehow Keith Fletcher and I got hold of the ball it was proposed we should use. It was dreadful and looked as though it had already been used several times. We thought that it should be thrown away and I threw it underarm, powerfully enough for it to reach the tunnel leading to the dressing room. An official standing in the tunnel picked it up, the umpires told him to bring it back and we had to use it. Ironically it began to swing about all over the place and Greig took 5 for 24 in 19.5 overs of great swing bowling. Having fielded all day in the extreme heat, I had just gratefully clambered into a bath back at the hotel when Dennis Amiss, who was rooming with me, said that the manager Donald Carr wanted to see me in his room immediately. I finished my bath and then went to see him to be strongly reprimanded for my behaviour.

In the next match against South Zone at Bangalore I batted number three and scored a career-best 156, which resulted in my moving up the order to that position in the remaining three Tests. It is doubtful whether that is the correct position for a wicket-keeper because he may not be in the right mental and physical condition to bat there after a long period in the field. My most successful Test innings have generally been when batting under pressure and lower down in the order.

We lost the third Test at Madras on a turning wicket, with Derek Underwood unable to play. He had sunstroke after sunbathing the day before the match and wasn't fit the next day, missing out on a spinner's paradise. It brought back an unhappy memory of Underwood on the under-25 tour to Pakistan in 1966–7. Having played on wonderful batting wickets, we arrived at Chittagong to find an ideal track for spin bowlers. Underwood and I were rooming together and he agreed with my request to have the fan on all night to combat the heat. When we woke up the next morning, his neck was so stiff he couldn't turn his head. So he had to watch Alan Ormrod, very much an occasional bowler, pick up five wickets, bowling spin on the only pitch which turned throughout the tour. Nor did I wake up unscathed myself – mosquitoes had penetrated the net and I was covered in bites, which required treatment with calamine lotion for days after.

It was in India's second innings at Madras, when they lost six wickets getting the 86 they required to win, that there was another incident. It was a bad wicket and we knew India would struggle. Their captain Ajit Wadekar edged a ball from Chris Old to be caught by Tony Greig at second slip. Wadekar stood his ground and we just couldn't believe it. It was a formality, we thought, in asking the umpire to give him out but he rejected our appeal. I flicked off one of my gloves a long way up in the air. It was a gesture of desperation but I realize now it was pure bad behaviour and certainly something I would hope not to do since becoming a Christian. The game is far better off without that kind of behaviour on the field, although I accept that players can get caught up in the excitement of the match, especially on the big occasion. Barry Wood, looking very upset, rushed towards the umpire. Tony Lewis also went over to the umpire, who eventually consulted his colleague at square leg, and finally Wadekar was given out. Why there was hesitation I cannot imagine, because it was a straightforward catch. Umpires can make mistakes but we players can too, of course, dropping catches or getting out when we shouldn't.

Following that day's play I had to see the manager again about my behaviour, which on that tour, I'm afraid to admit, was the worst in my career. I wasn't very happy about my conduct at Bombay in the fifth Test. In those days I sometimes used to swear badly, particularly when I got out. It was an umpire's decision which provoked me at Bombay – a very dubious one, which sent me back to the pavilion, swearing terribly and throwing down the bat when I got into the dressing room. I was on about umpires cheating, but with more experience I came to realize that their job is not easy, especially in India, with crowds of around 100,000 yelling at them, and this intense pressure can cause them to make mistakes. My view is that for several Test series there should be an experiment with neutral umpires. That could resolve many problems.

How lucky we have been in England to have such fine umpires. To do their job they have to love the game and when you talk to them you realize that they do. Two great umpires during my playing career have been David Constant and Dicky Bird. Constant was one of the coaches when I first went to Eltham Baths as an eleven-year-old. I used to earn a sixpence every time I got him out: he kindly used to get out deliberately. He always gave me tremendous encouragement when we played together in the county's second eleven. In recent years I have been able to help him in his bid to be one of the fittest umpires by supplying him with a list of the exercises that are used in our gymnasium. (He'll have to go some, however, to keep up with the fitness of Alan Whitehead and Barry Leadbeater, both regular runners.)

Cricket followers will probably always link Constant and me with an umpiring decision he gave against me in the 1980 Trent Bridge Test against the West Indies. I was amazed to see his finger raised in answer to a leg-before appeal from Malcolm Marshall. Bowling round the wicket, Marshall dug the ball in very short. It pitched well outside leg stump and struck me on the forearm. I felt it was missing off stump and high but Constant had a different view. Even the 'greats' are human and can make a mistake.

To return to my point about bad behaviour, I think it is true that in sport generally the language can be pretty bad and although mine used to be, I tried never to swear again after I became a Christian. The fact that other people do is their choice, although it was disappointing to hear Dennis Lillee, who has always been one of my heroes, really having a go at me in Sydney during the 1974–5 tour. The luck was going my way and he was directing his swearing at me all the time. I must admit I was very surprised, but when he did it again at the Oval in 1981 I was more prepared to take no notice of it. However, as soon as the day's play was over, he was one of the first to mix with the opposition and forget about what happened on the field – as great an ambassador off the field as he was a competitor on it.

Perhaps swearing is an indication of the great pressures players are under today to win. I think, though, that playing as well as possible for your side and giving every ounce of energy and concentration is the right approach. That will supply entertainment. Let the result take care of itself: that is the healthiest attitude for a cricketer. Many players become so involved in the result that nerves can take over. You should accept that cricket is a game which sometimes you will lose. I try not to mind whether we lose or win; the only time I would get upset is if I felt I hadn't tried hard enough. If you have tried your utmost and things still don't go right for you, there's nothing else you can do about it.

# Six

# Caribbean Trouble

Ray Illingworth, having missed the winter tour, regained the captaincy when the three-match series against New Zealand began in the summer of 1973. The first match was tremendous and the Kiwis might have won if Bev Congdon had not got out just before the close on the fourth day. He had batted nearly seven hours and I think it was exhaustion which brought about his dismissal.

In the second Test I registered my first 'pair' in first-class cricket – and it had to be at international level and at Lord's! The only previous time I had bagged the dreaded pair was when playing for Kent schools, trapped leg-before, a dubious decision, as I was playing my favourite sweep shot against Richard Burnett (the grandson of Frank Woolley). So at Lord's I had plenty of time to sit back and enjoy Keith Fletcher's 178, one of the best innings I have seen him play. It was a great shame that he was in and out of the England side, because, as his record proves, he certainly had the ability required at Test level. It seemed to be a tradition of the England selectors to play people for a couple of Tests and then drop them. Dennis Amiss suffered the same sort of experience as Fletcher and it cannot be good for a player's confidence. The Australians, however, in those days would pick a player and then stand by him, allowing him a long run. Paul Sheahan would be in that category and yet his Test record (1594 runs at 33.91) was not as good as that of Amiss (3612 runs at 46.30) or Fletcher (3272 runs at 39.90). If Fletcher had been given a fair run in the England side, instead of being in and out, he might have enjoyed a much better career and would have played many more than the fifty-nine Tests he did.

An enthusiastic person, he has been a very good county captain for Essex, with the happy knack of getting the best out of his players, and has been one of the best catchers close in on the off-side. His captaincy can be very defensive, using the rules of the game to the full in championship cricket. I remember facing John Lever, then an England bowler, who took the new ball without a slip fielder, and I wasn't even off the mark. But when it is necessary to attack, there is none better than Fletcher in the modern game.

Fletcher had been a very good friend since we roomed together on our first tour with the Cavaliers. We both returned from the 1969 tour of Pakistan to be married – his wedding was the day after mine, so we were unable to attend each other's ceremonies. He was involved in an amusing incident while batting in a double-wicket competition in South Africa. He snicked a ball from Bev Congdon to be caught by me behind the wicket. He didn't walk though and the umpire turned down the appeal. He had always walked when I had caught him in county cricket and I asked him why he hadn't on this occasion. He replied, 'I didn't know where to walk.' Because of the competition rules the outgoing batsman either went to square leg or to the other end, allowing the non-striker to continue his innings.

It was one of Fletcher's colleagues at Essex, Keith Boyce, who played such a major role in our series defeat by the West Indies in the second half of the summer of 1973. What a fantastic series he enjoyed. One of my 'bogey' bowlers – Gary Gilmour and Ashley Mallett were among the others – Boyce really buzzed at Test level. He didn't bowl very quick all the time at county level but in Test cricket his adrenalin flowed and he bowled fast and with great skill. He had the uncanny knack of delivering a bouncer where the ball swung towards you or away from you after it had pitched. It was very unusual but it is an attribute sometimes displayed by another West Indian paceman, Sylvester Clarke, who plays for Surrey.

Boyce's opening partner in the attack was my county colleague, Bernard Julien. What a tragedy it was that his career over
here didn't last much longer for he was one of the finest players
Kent ever had, potentially the best all-rounder. He was a very
formidable new-ball left-arm bowler, swinging the ball in to the
right-hander, with a great line and length; he had the ability also
to bowl orthodox spin and wrist spin. He was one of the longest
throwers of a cricket ball I have ever seen; one of his achieve-
ments was to throw a ball from the far side of the square at
Canterbury back over the Frank Woolley stand, a massive effort.
A splendid all-round fielder, he won the 'Greatest Catch' prize in
the first season of World Series Cricket. He was with Kent in their
heyday, which meant, unfortunately for him, he tended to bat at
number nine, yet he was capable of scoring hundreds at Test
level. He was wasted in the one-day competitions with Kent
because he never consistently batted high enough up the order.
Granted it was a very difficult problem for a captain, healthy
though it was, to decide where to bat Julien. He had available
Denness, Luckhurst, Asif, Cowdrey, Shepherd, Julien, Knott,
Woolmer – eight Test players, and Alan Ealham and Graham
Johnson to be fitted in too.

There was some memorable batting by the West Indies during
that series. Rohan Kanhai played magnificently in the third Test
at Lord's but his best innings in my view was the century he
scored for Warwickshire off the Kent attack at Gravesend in 1970.
It was a rain-affected wicket, ideal for Derek Underwood, but
Kanhai's opening shot was a straight-driven six off Underwood
over the sightscreen. He started as though he felt he would not be
at the crease very long because of the state of the wicket. Then,
having got going so well, he obviously decided that he would be
all right if he played properly. He did – and it was a really great
knock.

Sobers played brilliantly in that Lord's Test and Julien's century, the third of the innings, was scored batting at number eight.
It was one of the earliest opportunities he had at Test level of
showing what a really great all-rounder he was. How well he
grabbed it, playing some marvellous attacking shots, reaching his
century in two and a half hours.

It was during that Test, in England's first innings, that there
was a bomb scare. I was batting and we were told to stay out in

the middle, because it was the safest place. We just stood around and chatted as some eighty-five minutes' playing time was lost.

John Snow was dropped after the first Test at the Oval and it was strange to be in an England side without him for he was one of England's great fast bowlers at Test level. I liked him very much – he was thoughtful, a great person to talk to, because he was very interesting and reckoned that there were other things in life apart from cricket. He could be aggressive and you could always tell that mood because his lips went bluey-white when he was annoyed. His great quality was that he controlled his anger, and it probably made him a better and quicker bowler. He had been involved in an incident with Sunil Gavaskar, the Indian batsman, at Lord's in 1971. Live, it looked very harmless but in slow motion on the television it seemed as though Snow had shoulder-charged him. It was half playful really, but of course it was blown up by the media and people were always trying to label Snow a 'bad boy'. He was dropped for the second Test as a disciplinary measure, which was very unfair. During the tea interval Billy Griffith, then secretary of the MCC, came into our dressing room and criticized Snow in very strong terms. Illingworth very quickly asked Mr Griffith to leave the dressing room, making it clear that he didn't want his players distracted at what was a very important stage in the match – we only wanted two more wickets to win it but India had a slight chance of winning too. Mr Griffith left as soon as he was asked.

His son Mike and I had come up together through second-eleven and festival cricket, but unfortunately Mike stopped wicket-keeping, possibly because he played for Sussex, who already had Jim Parks. Cricket is an amazing game – there are so many people with talent who don't make it to the top. Mike Griffith as a young player was one you would have thought should have played for England as a wicket-keeper/batsman. So many people you think will make it don't, and the same applies in reverse. Luck plays an important part – producing the right performance at the right time is vital, because then you may be given an opportunity. Mr Griffith had encouraged my wicket-keeping and was always ready to chat about it. I particularly remember him telling me how well he thought I had kept on a bad wicket at Lord's in 1969 against New Zealand. It was a great boost from an ex-England 'keeper.

At the end of the 1973 series against the West Indies Illingworth lost the captaincy. It seemed as though the administrators were just looking for one mistake and our 2–0 defeat gave them their chance. Ironically, my next game after the final Test was for Kent at Folkestone – against Leicestershire, led by Illingworth. It was a slightly embarrassing situation for me because my county captain, Mike Denness, was taking over from the man whom I and many other players had not wanted to see lose the job, a man whom I regard as the best captain I played under at Test level, even above Mike Brearley who I rate as a superb captain.

We opened our sports shop in 1973 in Herne Bay. Jan's twin brother Alan and his wife Linda helped a great deal (by the way, they have twin daughters, so you can see twins are in the family) and a few months later Alan decided to come and manage the shop for us. With all the travel I'm involved in playing cricket at home and abroad you can imagine how relieved Jan and I felt to know that Alan was looking after the business; he's really ideal for the trade as he loves all sports, especially squash. Linda now does the book-keeping, having taken over from Major Bert Crowder who was assistant secretary for many years at Kent County Cricket Club during Les Ames's reign as manager and secretary. He must like Kent wicket-keepers! When we first thought of opening the shop I was also greatly indebted to the advice of former Sussex bowler Tony Buss, who had a similar business.

Our fortune against the West Indies did not change when we met again in the first Test of the 1973–4 tour at Port of Spain. The match, which they won by seven wickets, will be remembered by many for the last ball of the second day's play when Alvin Kallicharran was run out in most unusual circumstances. Derek Underwood was the bowler, Bernard Julien the batsman, and Kallicharran, on 142, was at the non-striker's end, which was furthest away from the pavilion. Julien played the ball out on to the off-side. Thinking that that was the end of play for the day I followed my natural reaction, of taking the stumps out of the ground and delivering the bails to the square-leg umpire, who on that occasion was on the off-side of the wicket. As I was giving the bails to him there was a crash of wickets and an appeal. I said to the umpire, 'Has he been given out?' and he replied, 'Yes.' Then I saw the umpire at the bowler's end, Douglas Sang Hue, with his arm held high in the air. Tony Greig, fielding on the off-side, had apparently hurled the ball at the stumps and hit them. Meanwhile Kallicharran was halfway down the wicket, looking extremely annoyed. Leaving the pitch, it all seemed to be taken fairly light-heartedly, but back in the pavilion, apparently, officials of both sides were discussing it, with telephone calls being made to Lord's. It seemed to me that there was a hidden worry about the fact that Greig had been born in South Africa. My impression was that possibly England officials felt that for the future of the tour it would be good public relations to withdraw the appeal. That was the eventual decision and Kallicharran was allowed to continue his innings. The next day was a rest and when he resumed the following day, after he and Greig had shaken hands, he only added another sixteen runs. Technically I suppose Kallicharran was out that night and the umpire had no alternative but to give that decision, unless he had called 'over'. But my instincts told me that the ball was dead and the game was over for the day, and indeed it was suggested that my action in removing the bails was premature. Julien had already turned and started walking towards the pavilion, so there could be no suggestion that Kallicharran was looking for a run. The possible lesson to be learned is that in those circumstances it might be safer for the non-striking batsman, if he is backing up, to return and touch his bat in the crease. If the ball had missed the stumps and gone for four overthrows would there have been any argument about the runs being recorded?

Kingston, Jamaica, was the venue for the second Test, which we drew thanks to a magnificent innings of 262 by Dennis Amiss, following his 174 in the first Test. Some people have occasionally questioned whether Amiss was a player of Test standard, but that is truly ridiculous. His record has proved them wrong and he should have played 100 Tests. He was a player who, once he had scored 50, always looked as if he could go on to make a very big score. We were room-mates in Jamaica and Antigua and in that second Test when I was struggling hard to hold my Test place, after a loss of form, he ran me out. He played a ball to cover and Clive Lloyd, then at his peak fielding in that position, ran me out when Amiss called for a single. It was a blow for me because I needed to score runs and amazingly there was a repeat performance when we played our next match in Antigua. Batting at number three to have the opportunity to play an innings, I was again partnering Amiss, who played the ball into the covers and called for a single. A youngster we had not seen much of before moved like a flash to pick up the ball and throw down the stumps, running me out by yards. His name – Viv Richards. I remember saying, 'Oh no, not again!' as we passed one another in the middle of the wicket. Being such good friends we were able to joke about it. Fortunately, when I went in to bat in the next match, which was the Barbados Test, he was already out so I had a chance to get a few runs!

In the third Test at Bridgetown Amiss opened the innings with Mike Denness and Geoff Boycott moved down to number four, which set many people talking about the decision. I felt it was correct for Boycott to drop down. He was going through a spell where his hooking wasn't right. He was getting caught on the boundary and becoming indecisive about whether or not to play that shot. He was such a master batsman that it seemed a waste if the bounce of the new ball was to result in his dismissal. The wickets were exceptionally flat after the new ball had lost its bounce, so batting at number four, when it would probably be softer, Boycott would find it much easier to hook. Boycott understood the reasoning behind the move but he was a little worried about backing out of the firing line. He certainly didn't enjoy the experience of waiting to go in to bat. There was a similar decision in Australia for the Centenary Test in 1977, which saw Amiss drop down to number four and Bob Woolmer open. I was one of the four selectors on that tour and was strongly in favour of the switch. The reason was similar – not to waste Amiss against the new ball. Possibly he should have batted at number four for England throughout his career.

It was after the second Test in the West Indies that I decided to alter my batting stance. In England in the second half of the previous season I had had a hard time against the West Indies, struggling to play the quick bowlers, especially Keith Boyce. I was getting hit on the gloves or in the chest; something had to be done if they were going to bowl at that height all the time. Standing in front of a mirror and looking at the bowler's target area – between my head and my waist – I lifted up the bat to cover it. It was immediately obvious that in that position the grip was completely different – the top hand was much further round the back of the bat and the bottom hand was holding the bat with forefinger and thumb. What really persuaded me to make the alteration was that it was much easier to get the bat up high with this new grip and a more open stance. I had always followed Geoff Boycott's early advice about going back and across to the quick bowlers, but now I decided just to stand still behind the batting crease with the more open stance. I tried it for the first time in the match against Barbados, when some of the selectors might have been considering dropping me. Fortunately I did get selected for the Test and scored 87 and 67, under pressure in both innings, and we just about saved the match. I have batted against the quick bowlers with that grip and open stance with slight modifications ever since and it has certainly helped me.

Before the third Test at Barbados I picked up a bat belonging to Dennis Amiss and reckoned it was just the one I would like to use. Amiss said I could borrow it but it needed logo stickers so Bob Taylor, a signwriter by profession, made the necessary changes – the man waiting to replace me if I was dropped assisting me to prepare the bat with which I saved my Test place.

It was in that Test that Andy Roberts made his debut. There was also the innings of 302 from Lawrence Rowe. It was one of the greatest I have seen. What a tragedy that eye trouble hindered his career. How good would he have been? In the same match, even if only for a short spell in his career, Tony Greig emerged as the best off-spinner I have ever seen in Test cricket. He had bowled off-cutters well in Jamaica and his off-spin in the rest of the series was quite fantastic. When you batted against him in the nets you didn't know how you could survive. He got bounce and really spun the ball, giving you the feeling that you were always going to be caught by a close fielder. He had been bowling out-swingers but their effect was countered by the presence of so many left-handers in the West Indies line up – Roy Fredericks, Kallicharran, Lloyd and Sobers. So Greig said that he would try something different and turned to off-cutters and then to off-spin. He took 6 for 164 in forty-two overs of off-spin, while Pat Pocock had 0 for 93 in twenty-eight overs, during the match. The climax of Greig's development as an off-spinner came in the final Test at Trinidad where his phenomenal performance helped us to win the match and square the series 1–1, when we might well have lost three Tests. In that last Test he outbowled Derek

Underwood on a turning wicket, taking 8 for 86 and 5 for 70, bowling sixty overs in the match.

It seemed at Trinidad, with the West Indies needing 226 to win and starting the last day 30 for no wicket, that it was a reasonably even contest, with the odds slightly in their favour. The important wicket was that of Gary Sobers. The answer to our query about how we were going to get him out arrived out of the blue. He suddenly played over a very full-length ball from Underwood and was bowled. That really swung the game our way. Eventually it was with great relief that we saw the arrival of Lance Gibbs at the wicket. He wasn't the best of tail-enders and we had just taken the new ball, with the West Indies at 197 for 9. Two runs later he was bowled by Geoff Arnold and we had won the match. Gibbs, as I have said, was one of the greatest off-spinners; he was an outstanding catcher too, specializing in the gully, where he caught me off John Shepherd during the 1969 season in this country. It was a fantastic effort, diving away to his left to clutch the ball in one of those enormous hands with the very long fingers which obviously gave him the added ability to spin the ball.

The end of the tour was an especially happy time. My wife Jan and I had enjoyed the stay in Georgetown, Guyana, from where we had flown up to the jungle and visited the Kaiatura Falls and Johnson's Leap, where we found a pressed flower to bring back for Graham Johnson's wife Marion because we knew she collected them. On the way home there were matches in Bermuda but I was given time off from most of the cricket and we spent another ten days on the island to enjoy a holiday after the MCC party had left.

Back in England we won the three-match series easily against India. The second Test series of the summer against Pakistan was tighter but rain intervened on the two occasions a result was possible. At Headingley no play was possible on the final day, which could have been very close because we wanted 44 to win with only four wickets in hand and Keith Fletcher the only specialist batsman left – on 67 not out.

Then at Lord's we wanted only 60 to win on the last day with all our wickets in hand, but again no play was possible. It seemed to everyone in the England camp that we should have been out there playing, but no apparent effort was made to remove the covers or dry out the ground. It was as if the authorities were embarrassed about the water getting on to the pitch earlier in the match – leaving a situation for Derek Underwood to exploit so handsomely. He took 5 for 20 and 8 for 51 but the ball only turned when he bowled over the wicket and Wasim Bari showed how to combat him by padding up to deliveries pitched outside the leg stump. It was like turning back the clock to see Underwood in action because in his early years he had always bowled over the wicket. On that frustrating fifth day we were not even allowed to go out on to the ground, let alone into the middle to see what the pitch was like.

It was a good end to the summer for Kent because we won the Gillette Cup, beating Lancashire in the final at Lord's. There was no play on the Saturday because of rain and we had to go to Worcester on the Sunday, where we were beaten in a John Player League match. Back at Lord's on the Monday, we triumphed over Lancashire in a low-scoring game and I was presented with the Man of the Match award by Brian Close, my first England captain. (My 19 must be one of the lowest scores to win that award!) It was the second such award in succession because in the semi-final against Somerset at Canterbury I had received it, my first ever in the cup competitions, from Ken Barrington, who was my number-one choice as the best batsman, as a run-getter, produced by England. His Test record – 6806 runs in eighty-two matches for an average of 58.67 speaks for itself. A very amusing and genuinely nice person, he retained those qualities to become an excellent tour manager in India in 1976–7. As a manager he had the priceless quality of being very interested in how people played. He became very involved in the matches, as though he were actually playing. He invariably practised with the boys and he appreciated how hard the game had become, especially with the barrage of fast bowlers. Wally Grout, the great Australian wicket-keeper, once said that when Barrington went out to bat you could see the Union Jack fluttering behind him.

# Seven

# Greatest Friend

The summer of 1974 saw the visits of India and Pakistan, but for me those two series were completely overshadowed by my becoming a Christian.

Prayer had first come into my life when I was a young lad. I used to have dreadful nightmares, which caused me problems in getting to sleep. At one school Christmas service there were prayers ending: 'Through Jesus Christ our Lord, Amen'. I can remember lying in bed one night praying that I would not have those nightmares. They stopped and I prayed every night from then on, ending with the words I had learned from that Christmas service. My feeling was that, if there was a God, by praying I was putting money in the bank, as it were – that if there was a God he might look on me kindly because of my prayers. That really was as far as my Christian thoughts went until the winter of 1971–2.

That was a free winter for me. We had always wanted to go to Acapulco, and Jan and I decided that on the way we would take up the offer of an American, Dr Clifford Severn, whom I had met in England and become friendly with, to go to California and do some coaching. So we went early in 1972, staying with Dr Severn's daughter Vonnie, her husband Roy Shelley and their son Billy who were Christians. It introduced us to a Christian life within a family. We saw how they lived and how the Lord was in their life. On the last evening of our week's stay, one of Mrs Shelley's brothers, who was a pastor, paid a visit. That was my first meeting with Billy Severn. We all chatted and then prayed. It was my first experience of someone suggesting that Jesus Christ could come into the lives of Jan and myself. We didn't really give a great deal more thought to that evening but in the summer of 1972 Billy Severn and his wife Barbara visited England. We met up with them in London where Christianity cropped up in the course of our conversations. I shall never forget one of our evenings. It was in the restaurant at the top of the Post Office Tower in London where they were our guests at dinner. This was my first visit so I wasn't sure of the prices. Californian strawberries were a popular choice, but they boosted the cost of the meal substantially. When the bill arrived I hadn't enough money and had to go to my car to get my cheque book – quite a journey when you are at the top of what was then the tallest building in London!

Billy had been an American footballer and quite a useful cricketer. In fact all his family were – his father 'Doc' Severn had played the game in California with C. Aubrey Smith, who captained England in his only Test during the 1888–9 tour of South Africa. Billy came one day to the Oval during practice before the Test against the Australians and bowled in the nets. He was all dressed to fly home later that day and departed with grass stains and mud on his trousers after slipping over at the end of his long run. Before he left he introduced me at the Oval to a friend, Eldin Corsie, who was pastor at the Kensington Temple.

At the end of the 1973 season Kent were scheduled to tour Canada. I had decided not to make the trip but when Alan Ealham dropped out I was asked to reconsider and agreed to go if the county would organize that Jan and I could fly on from Canada to California, where we could visit the Shelley and Severn families again. So we went to Canada and then on to California, where the discussions with Billy Severn on Christianity were resumed. Were the doubts lessening in my mind? On the last day of our stay Billy said, 'Don't go away from California without what you really came for.' He was suggesting that we had only returned for one reason – to bring the Lord into our lives. Knowing how I had been thinking, Billy suggested that

instead of trying to prove that God didn't exist I should switch to
the opposite viewpoint – I should believe that God did exist until
someone could prove otherwise – and if I did I would discover
that nobody could persuade me that God did not exist. He felt it
would be a great idea for me to take time to think about
Christianity and that travelling by car around the country to play
cricket could provide an ideal opportunity to do so.

By the summer of 1974 I was giving Christianity a great deal of
thought. In July there was a telephone call while we were visiting
Jan's parents in Northfleet to say that her older brother Brian had
been involved in an extremely serious car-crash in Wales.
Immediately I drove his wife Linda and Jan to Aberystwyth.
During the seven hours' drive I prayed that Brian would be all
right. We went straight to the hospital where we were told that he
might not live and that if he did he might suffer permanent brain
damage. Everybody was very concerned and worried about his
condition but as soon as I saw him I somehow seemed to know
that he would pull through. He did make a very dramatic
recovery and was out of hospital within six weeks.

During that summer there was a sudden development in the
legal proceedings in which Ray Illingworth and myself had been
involved with Denis Compton and the *Sunday Express* newspaper
following an article written by Compton concerning our tour of
Australia in 1970–1. Our financial backer in the litigation had
dropped out and when I telephoned our solicitor I was told that if
we pursued the libel case on our own it could cost us £40,000 each
if we lost. That was an awful lot of money but it was a very
involved case, which would mean people travelling from
Australia to give evidence. I prayed a great deal about all that,
and eventually, out of the blue, I received a call from the
solicitor's office to be told: 'We've got some great news – the
*Sunday Express* have decided to settle out of court and pay costs.'

It was an unbelievable relief to me and so in a very short space
of time I had two examples of the power of prayer. I was
beginning to realize that Jesus Christ was becoming very important in my life. The feeling was growing so strong in me to return
to the Kensington Temple, which we had been visiting occasionally that summer. On previous visits we had seen people walking
forward to become Christians. I am not saying that it is necessary
to give your life to the Lord by going to Church and walking

forward in front of a congregation, but I was sure on this occasion that I would be taking that action. When the invitation was extended for people to go forward, I just turned to Jan and said I had to go. I went and she followed me and I think that Eldin Corsie, who was conducting the service, had known all along that we would one day be taking this step, although he did not realize that we were there that night. We chatted together after the service and Jan mentioned how disappointed she was about not having had a baby, although we had been trying for a number of years. Eldin suggested we should pray about it, and we did. Not long after, before the end of October in fact, when I was in Australia, I received a telephone call to say that Jan was pregnant.

So becoming a Christian was a gradual process for me: from praying every night when I was young to my visits to California and seeing the joy in the Christians we met there; from my talks with Billy Severn up to my visits to Eldin Corsie and the Kensington Temple. My relationship with the Lord isn't something that can be switched on and off just to gain results when I need to. In fact, for me prayer means continual contact with the Lord. It is wonderful knowing the story and message of Jesus Christ, to know that the Lord is with you every moment of your life. He knows and shares every thought and feeling you have; He is your greatest friend. I don't feel that you have to go on your knees to pray. Sometimes I will because it feels the natural thing to do, but I can pray just as easily on my way out to bat. I wouldn't pray that I would score runs but for the safety of the other players and myself, and that I would have the appetite to try 100 per cent.

The comfort you get from being a Christian was brought home to me on 1 October 1983, when I received news of the death of Andy Rogers, one of Jan and my greatest friends, whom I had first met at a cocktail party in Australia in 1970–1. He was one of the most natural, warm and funny people you could meet. He had so much zest for life, and the most open personality I have come across, with so much interest in and care about other people's lives. Throughout his funeral I could imagine him looking down on us and wanting us to be happy rather than sad. I knew that we were going to miss him greatly, but we could rejoice that he was going to be with the Lord in a place of so much peace and joy. It is always hard for those left behind, but we should not be mean in wanting our loved ones to be with us rather than with our Creator.

If you are a Christian you are able to leave situations in the Lord's hands and that brings a perfect contentment. An example of this was the decision to go on the South African tour. The Lord knew that I wanted to go and that I thought it was right for me to do so. I prayed that if it wasn't right He would prevent me from going, or that if it wasn't right for the tour to go ahead He would stop it from taking place. I knew that even when we arrived in South Africa the tour could still be called off.

Another example of the Lord's guidance came for me, as I have already explained, with my decision to sign for WSC.

But prayer is not, of course, merely for personal guidance. A great deal of my prayers are for other people, whether for a minor ailment or a major problem. And when those prayers are answered it brings such great happiness, not only to them but also to me, to experience the friendship and the love of the Lord.

# Eight

# Bouncers

We went to Australia in 1974–5 feeling fairly confident. We had played very well towards the end of the previous winter's tour of the West Indies, had comfortably beaten India at home and had had a moral victory over Pakistan. Of course, we realized that India can be reasonably easy to beat on English wickets. But on arrival in Australia we soon discovered that press reports of Jeff Thomson's speed were not exaggerated – he could really bowl quick. It brought back memories of the first time we had seen Lillee at Perth in 1970–1. Then, we all got up to look out of the dressing-room window and saw Lillee's first ball take Geoff Boycott's hat off. So in 1974–5 everybody soon knew Thomson would be a force to be reckoned with. After Lillee's first two overs in the series, we could see that Lillee himself was obviously as great a threat as ever. We knew that Australians had got out in the past against short-pitched bowling and in the first innings of the first Test at Brisbane we bounced four of them out on the first day. Mike Hendrick had Wally Edwards caught at fine leg off a bouncer; Greig certainly bounced out Lillee; Ian Chappell got a bouncer and was caught by Greig, bowled Willis; Doug Walters got one, caught Lever, bowled Willis; and so it went on. The next day Terry Jenner fell to a short ball to make it five.

There was no doubt that they were going to bowl aggressively and we fired the first shots. On that tour, as a pair, Lillee and Thomson were the fastest two I have ever seen and they were bowling on quick, uneven wickets. They were probably at their quickest by the fourth Test in Sydney. There Geoff Arnold received a ball from Lillee that missed his head by a whisker and he never moved. It went high over Rodney Marsh, first bounce into the sightscreen. Even Lillee looked relieved that it had not hit the batsman because if it had I don't know what would have happened. Those two bowlers were so quick and so fit, they bowled long spells without dropping their pace. Even at Sydney there were lighter moments. David Lloyd, of Lancashire, a very humorous chap, was sitting in the dressing room and pretended to write home to his mum. 'Dear Mum,' he wrote, 'Today I received a half volley.' He paused, and then added: 'In the nets.' During the same Test there was a big shout from Keith Fletcher in the front dressing room (there are two at Sydney): 'Hey, lads,' he said, 'the spinner's on.' We all rushed to see what was happening and there was the fast-medium Max Walker, just bowling an over so Thomson and Lillee could change ends. Fletcher it was who walked out to bat in the match to be greeted by Lillee. The two had been involved in an incident when Lillee, who was batting, had been hit on the arm. As Fletcher went out to bat now Lillee said, 'Good luck, Fletch, you're going to need it.' He duly got hit by Thomson, gloving a ball on to his head. It rebounded out as far as cover where Ross Edwards dropped the chance. Those, of course, were the days before helmets.

To my mind Thomson and Lillee in harness sparked off the beginning of a change of era in Test cricket. It was a time to add new ideas to batting technique. Looking back, I was extremely fortunate to be at the top of my batting form. My batting peak was from 1974 to 1977 and this tour coincided with that. When you are in good form you don't worry, because you are seeing the ball so clearly. But when you are out of touch and not seeing the ball it is a completely different game. Thomson's deliveries would take off even when pitched up. Out of form you would have had a nightmare of a time. My technique was to be ready to play the ball in front of my chest or head and leave as many deliveries as possible. I would wait for them to bowl slightly wide of off-stump so I could play the upper cut over slips and gully. Greig was the first batsman I had seen do that consistently in a Test match and he deservedly scored a century. If you didn't attempt to do something like this, Thomson and Lillee would simply run in on wickets which were not very good and gain the upper hand. Greig, on his way to that hundred, at one point cover-drove Lillee for four, and then got down on one knee and signalled the boundary. Then when the bouncers came he was pretending to head them away. That's the confident form he was in. I never felt he did this sort of thing in a nasty way. It was without malice and it was a great shame that at times the opposition misunderstood him, because his great quality was that he loved people and cricket. Playing those shots outside the off-stump was a necessity, otherwise you were going to stand there all day and not get any runs, because there were very few deliveries which you could drive. That is how I think the modern player would have played then. For instance, I cannot see Allan Lamb blocking it out all day. He would have gone for those sort of shots.

That tour was marked by two notable occurrences. The captain, Mike Denness, dropped himself from the fourth Test, an immensely difficult decision to make. He had been unwell at one stage but he had got over that. In the end, I suppose, it comes down to the fact that if you are the captain but you are not playing well and there are players of high calibre around, then you should not play. In that respect he made the right decision. The other famous event of that 1974–5 tour was the call-up to the squad of Colin Cowdrey. Dennis Amiss had his thumb broken by Thomson and John Edrich had a finger broken by Lillee in the first Test at Brisbane. Within a day or two of his arrival Cowdrey was going out to bat in the second Test in Perth. He was padded up with chest guards and so on. To one of the early deliveries he faced he turned to chest it away. But it climbed very high, just getting the top of his chest and nearly hitting his chin. He realized then what a struggle it was going to be. Cowdrey, of course, followed the old theory, trying to block it out. But he scored few runs and eventually succumbed. It was not long after his arrival in Australia that he turned to Tony Greig and said, 'You can't play them off, can you? They keep on roaring in.' During that first innings of Cowdrey's at the WACA ground there was a big shout from one spectator: 'Hey, Thommo,' it went, 'I've searched everywhere for a vet but can't find one. You put the old boy to sleep.' There had been similar treatment at Melbourne in the third Test during the 1970–1 tour and more jocular remarks when things were not going too well for Cowdrey in the slips. There were such comments as 'Cowdrey, shake your head, your eyeballs are stuck'. 'Colin, the media are trying to kid us England sent for you as a replacement, but we know the truth, you were deported' was another comment during the 1974–5 tour.

After the Sydney match on the 1974–5 tour, in which defeat meant we lost the Ashes, we moved on to Adelaide. Geoff Arnold bowled tremendously well with the new ball. But there was much criticism aimed at Mike Denness for not bringing on off-spinner Fred Titmus early enough. Doug Walters, one of the best players of off-spin, was not so good when the ball was swinging and seaming. Nevertheless he is the most entertaining batsman of all in my view. It was a wettish wicket and the ball turned for Derek Underwood, who took 7 for 113 and 4 for 102. Denness had a very difficult decision to make with Arnold bowling so well. Then when Titmus did come on the ball was not turning so much. It certainly isn't easy being a captain at times. Terry Jenner, in front of his home crowd, batted very well in the match, playing a vital knock of 74. Thomson was injured during that game while playing tennis on the rest day. It meant that Lillee, Max Walker and Ashley Mallett had to do most of the bowling. Australia bowled well and dismissed us for 241. We went into the last Test at Melbourne, the sixth of the series, and Thomson was out of their side. They brought in Geoff Dymock (not quite in the same pace bracket). Lillee broke down early on, which was a pity in a way because it would have been much more satisfying to win against their strongest team. In the event we won the match, Denness and Fletcher both getting centuries. Peter Lever was fit again and bowled brilliantly. I always thought the series could have been much different. Willis had fitness problems, Lever was affected by injury and the non-selection of John Snow was another great blow. Looking back on that tour I think how fortunate I was to be in decent batting form. Years later, during a World Series match, I remember watching some film of Lillee and Thomson bowling against us. There were very many frightening deliveries. I had gone through the series without wearing a helmet, chest guard, arm guard or inside thigh pad. Now I wear them all the time.

From Australia we went to New Zealand, as was still the

normal form with MCC teams in those days. On the last day of the first Test at Auckland in February 1975, I was keeping wicket when Ewan Chatfield received a dreadful blow on the head. He actually stopped breathing but was successfully given the kiss of life. Throughout the series in Australia we had played against Lillee and Thomson with the ball flying about at 90 miles an hour and people being hit because the wickets were very fast and at times had uneven bounce. Then at Auckland we had one of the slowest wickets you could expect to find at Test level. Comparing that wicket with those we had experienced in Australia, it was ironic that the bouncer from Peter Lever should hit Chatfield. For twenty minutes he had just been playing forward, and the bowler obviously thought a bouncer might make him play differently. It was so slow to rise that it was almost like a slow-motion replay. Chatfield, who was making his Test debut, had a habit of turning his head to the side and ducking so that his eyes were not on the ball at all. On this occasion he exposed his temple to the ball and it was just desperately unlucky that he was hit. When he turned, I saw that his face had actually collapsed on one side like dissolving wax. Next thing he was lying on the ground and because of his face I felt that he was in very serious trouble. In no time at all, Bernard Thomas, the England physio, and the first-aider were on the scene. We were asked to move away to give room and it seemed to be a matter of whether he was going to be resuscitated. Then the players were asked to clear the pitch. Lever was terribly distressed, holding his head in his hands. Chatfield was still lying there with Thomas and the first-aider. When we were standing outside the dressing room some of the New Zealand team asked how Chatfield was. I replied that he could be dead and their horrified reaction brought tears to my eyes. I went into our dressing room and cried. Chatfield had been given the kiss of life by Thomas and taken straight to hospital.

What joy and relief when we heard that he was breathing again. It seemed ridiculous that someone could have been killed like that when we were seeking just one wicket to win the match with a whole day in which to do it. When you are immersed in a game you don't give a thought to any such injury occurring. Having seen the Chatfield incident I am very pleased that helmets are now so much part of the game, especially for tail-end batsmen and close fielders. You only need to lose sight of the ball once in your career, make the wrong movement, point your temple in line and it could be your unlucky day. Some batsmen still don't wear helmets – it is true that they take a little while to get accustomed to. It affected my game a lot when I first started using one. You would not think it a great weight but it does influence the movement and position of your head, tilting your head slightly sideways so your eyes are not level with the ground. That means your head is not upright and it gives you an unnatural sight of the ball. Your position, in other words, is not the right one. I first sported a helmet in the first year of World Series Cricket, taking it off because I could not get used to the weight. That particular piece of headgear covered my ears and I felt as if I were in a different world. It reduced my concentration, my hearing wasn't so sharp and the visor seemed to impede my vision. I tried one without a visor and still I didn't enjoy it. Then I experimented, making up my own and wearing it under my hat. Mike Brearley had conceived the idea of wearing a skull-cap on similar lines. It was much lighter but extremely hot, too much so for comfort. I wore that type of headgear in 1980 against the West Indies, then had a light helmet made in Australia, which I've worn since.

There have been some serious injuries in first-class cricket. Roger Davies of Glamorgan was hit on the head fielding at bat and pad. Others have been injured, perhaps not quite so seriously but badly enough. I saw John Dyson on television at Adelaide when he was hit on the chest and collapsed. John Emburey hurried over and banged him hard on the chest as a first-aid measure. David Bailey, who used to play for Lancashire and played in glasses, was hit by a bouncer from Kent's Alan Brown some years ago and very badly cut his nose, which was broken and pushed to one side. Brian Close was hit on the forehead, again by Brown, who was then batting, at Gravesend. It could have gone for six. Everybody asked 'Closey' if he was all right, and he said, 'Come on, let's get on with the game.' He was lucky; he just rubbed his head and carried on fielding. Stuart Leary got a bad one on the head at Gravesend too when he was fielding at short leg against Northants. It looked terrible but Stuart, who was one of the funniest yet most competitive of sportsmen, joked, 'Ooh, my looks.' I am amazed but very thankful that no one has died in professional cricket over the years with bat-and-pad fielders – and batsmen too – being hit so regularly. It must average out that twice a week someone receives a dangerous blow. At least with helmets the chance of a fatal accident is that much less. Without them now you could have ambulances coming to every game.

Many people say bat-and-pad fielders get too close but I reckon they are safer closer in. The greatest fielders I have seen there at county level were Mickey Stewart and Mike Edwards at Surrey, and of course they didn't wear helmets. What they did have was that very good technique of covering their head with arms and hands when an attacking shot was played. Nowadays such fielders are wearing helmets, arm guards, shin pads and of course, as always, a box. But it is also knee pads they need because that's where protection is essential. Bat-and-pads certainly field deeper today: Edwards and Stewart got exceptionally close. Some argue you can see the ball come off the bat better if you are a bit further away. But edges on to pads which drop down the wicket are rarely caught now – Edwards and Stewart would have picked them up.

The close positions vary. At silly point, for example, there is not so much chance of being hit on the head as there is at short leg. The ball is not clipped up so much on the off-side and if you watch silly points they tend to stand up high when an attacking shot is played so any knocks will be taken on the legs, or at least on the lower part of the body. Keith Fletcher is marvellous there. I do not subscribe to the view that silly point is an intimidating position; it has developed through tactics. Let's face it, you get plenty of snicks there off pads, partly because people have changed their batting style. When playing with bat behind pad the catching chance tends to go out on the off-side. Certainly, wickets can be picked up in the close positions – quite often early in an innings batsmen get a nick on to their pads. But that does not alter the fact that it is an especially difficult place to field. I don't feel pressure with the field close in, on- or off-side, because that means there are gaps elsewhere through which to score runs. I do prefer them to wear a helmet because of the chance of hitting them as I play an attacking shot.

Brian Close, a very nice chap, was also a cricketer of unbelievable courage. He used to say that pain was in the mind. Once, close in, he was hit very hard by the Pakistani batsman, Ibadulla.

Next ball he was walking in on him. Ibadulla gave a little push
forward and after he had made contact with the ball Close was
touching him on the arm just to let him know that the blow had
had no effect. That was in my first Test, at which time Close's
fielding, particularly on rain-affected wickets, was incredible.
Later in the same match Majid Khan pushed forward to Derek
Underwood and played the ball in the middle, but Close just
walked forward from silly point, caught the ball and tossed it in
the air. Called back to play for England in 1976, he and John Edrich
had to open the batting. The West Indian bowlers were very
dangerous. It was gloomy and the dampness in the air livened
the wicket. On a bad pitch their fast bowlers were lethal. They
seemed out to soften us up and they gave us a real roasting. One
has to accept that nowadays in cricket bouncers are commonplace. I have watched film of the 'bodyline' series and heard old
players talk about it. It seems less aggressive compared with what
goes on in modern cricket. I can recall many occasions in recent
years: the Thomson and Lillee series against England, the West
Indians that night at Old Trafford in 1976, and even the West
Indians last summer, when much of the bowling was sustained
aggression. Cricketers who have been born into this era have not
experienced the quieter days of years gone by. I remember Les
Ames mentioning that he was shocked if he received more than
five bouncers a season. Even when I first started, if you ducked a
bouncer you did not get another because the theory was that it
was a waste of time and energy to bowl one to a non-hooker. In
county cricket bouncers at one time were limited to one an over,
but that could cause problems to a young batsman because when
he graduates into Test cricket from county cricket he begins to
play in a game where there are no limitations. In Test cricket he
will find himself receiving perhaps four bouncers an over and he
won't know how to deal with them because he has not had the
experience. This has got to be controlled by the umpires, who
must decide whether a bowler, rather than trying to dismiss the
batsman with a set plan, is merely delivering bouncers for the
purposes of intimidation.

The problem is that pace bowlers now are so strong and they
deliver their bouncers so well that it is difficult to tell what is a
bouncer and what is an 'effort' ball. By 'effort' ball I mean the
bowler really hitting the deck very hard to make the ball lift,

possibly off a length. Someone like Sylvester Clarke can bowl you a ball which you have to play in front of your chest. It might have been an attempted bouncer or it could have been an 'effort' ball. Umpires and batsmen have an enormous problem with wickets of uneven bounce, now commonplace, and an intended bouncer instead of rising to head height, as it was supposed to do, comes to the batsman at waist height. In contrast a good-length ball intended to rise to hip height can fly towards the chest. When I first started playing, the bouncer was a really short ball which lifted well over your head, but of course the wickets were truer then. Now it is aimed somewhere between your chest and your head. Umpires have got to be the arbitrators but I feel it can become an artificial game if you limit bouncers to one an over. Under that old law I have seen batsmen in county cricket, after receiving the one bouncer in the over, look to go forward to the next ball. It means that batsmen can take some liberties.

In my early days it was almost unheard of for a tail-ender to receive a bouncer, but nowadays they find they have to face their fair share. This of course can be very dangerous, but helmets help to protect them. Perhaps they find themselves being bounced because they have improved defensively as batsmen and are more able to hang around at the end of an innings. On the other hand there is a theory that with tail-enders wearing helmets the fast bowler might feel that he can bowl bouncers because the batsman has more chance of being saved from serious injury. So the fast bowler uses his full armoury against the nine, ten and jack, and that includes the short-pitched ball. He is aiming not to hit, I hope, but to make the batsman play differently, to play back instead of forward for example. What could be more frustrating than a tail-ender at Test level coming in to bat and pushing a long way forward before the ball is bowled? If you can make him start to hesitate about what he should do you must have a far greater chance of getting him out than if he can play forward without worry at receiving a short delivery. In the modern game fast bowlers have largely come to appreciate that if they are bowling bouncers all the time to batsmen they have to be prepared to receive some back.

Geoff Boycott is a batsman who has received his share of bouncers in his time and I think that in his mid-forties he still shows great determination and technique against real pace.

There is no doubt that he is in the very top group of fit players in county cricket. He is a credit to the game in that respect – he trains extremely hard, looks after himself and watches what he eats and drinks. He scored a century against Kent at Sheffield back in the 1983 season and it was a high-class one. He followed that up with another hundred at Tunbridge Wells in 1984 when I dropped him in the 40s. He is not perhaps the most natural athlete and he has to work very hard at his fitness. In that Sheffield match he proved he has still got the right technique. Graham Dilley, bowling very quickly, hit him in the face before he had scored but Geoff shrugged it off, battled on and reached his century.

He has always been a battler. He has had the problems of wearing glasses and then of contact lenses, but he has overcome them. Wearing contact lenses he often got dust behind the lens. Quite often you will see him pause, holding the bowler up while he does the cleaning work, and I have seen him get out on two or three occasions the ball after he has performed this operation. I warned him about that and it has become a source of humour between us. Now when I see him fiddling with his lens in games between Kent and Yorkshire, I might say, 'Next ball's your last, Fiery,' and he'll just smile and make sure he blocks the next delivery out.

He has always worked hard on technique for the game he loves playing. When his Test career started he struggled technically because he played so low and well forward, especially against the quick bowlers, and was frequently being hit on the hands. But it did not stop him getting runs. He adapted, however, and on his friendly and expert advice I adapted my batting too. For example, when we were in the England side in the early days he stressed the value against pace bowlers of taking the right foot back and across before the ball was bowled. I took that advice and years later I adapted my final technique from this.

Geoff and I have always been friendly but obviously since World Series Cricket and our very limited number of games together we have seen far less of each other. He is a very sensitive person and that means that occasionally he can get hurt very easily and perhaps react sometimes to things which might not worry other people, but that sensitivity, when channelled in another direction, makes him a very friendly, warm person with a special brand of humour. At times he has thought the world is against him but I am sure he has quite liked that and responded to it by being terribly determined to be successful. He has been keen to take the world on and prove something. I can remember stories that as a young pro people said he couldn't play: that only made him all the more tenacious. I owe him a great deal for his encouragement of my batting throughout my career.

# Nine

# Benefit of the Doubt

The first ever World Cup one-day competition was staged in England in 1975 and it started badly for me when I broke a finger in the first tie – against India at Lord's. It was a delivery from Tony Greig, down the leg-side, which I caught awkwardly, and the middle finger of my left hand was chipped. For the new competition the squads had to be named in advance, with no replacements allowed, so I was obliged to play on, but it was very uncomfortable. Moreover, it hardly seemed necessary for me to have played at Edgbaston against East Africa in the third game, because John Jameson could easily have kept wicket, as he had quite often done so for his county. More importantly, my wife Jan was in labour and in fact I returned from Birmingham direct to the Kent and Canterbury hospital, which stands adjacent to the St Lawrence cricket ground, having been told that my son James had been born. Our interest in the World Cup ended in the semi-final at Headingley when we were knocked out by Australia in a low-scoring game. It was a very close contest and we might have won it if we had held our catches. Gary Gilmour did the damage for Australia in perfect bowling conditions – the wicket was green and the weather overcast. He bowled well but it was ridiculous that there was no sightscreen at the end from which he was bowling his left-arm pace over the wicket. Everybody, including me, seemed to get out leg before. It was very difficult to pick up his deliveries, but even with a sightscreen he might well have been successful because he bowled so well in those conditions. In the final the West Indies beat Australia in an exciting encounter which really saw the start of international one-day cricket being taken seriously.

It was in the first Test at Edgbaston that Graham Gooch made his Test debut and bagged a pair. You could see he might struggle with his weight, a taller version of the young Rod Marsh. In fact, in his schools cricket he kept wicket and in one game for Essex schools batted number eleven. My mother always sent plenty of sweets to the Test matches I played in, and if Graham was in the side they were gone in a flash. He certainly has a sweet tooth, but what an example he is to the young cricketer. He has learnt to train extremely hard and he is always in peak condition. He has a great balance of trying 100 per cent on the pitch and enjoying the game to the full. He is one of, if not the, most exciting English batsmen of our time; I have even felt that there was a greater buzz at the mention of his name than at Dexter's.

That Test at Edgbaston proved to be the end of Mike Denness's reign as England captain. We lost the match after the Australians had been put in to bat but I still think that he made the right decision. Having played so many times at Edgbaston where it used to be a belter of a wicket, I appreciated that if you had the chance to put the opposition in because of weather conditions you should take it. On this occasion it was cloudy and overcast and having dismissed them for 320 we might then have enjoyed two sunny days, scored 500 and won the match. The tragedy for Denness and for England was that we had a thunderstorm and torrential rain. It is quite unfair that one side should win a game only because the ground has been flooded. The Australians, not having appreciated the rule about no covers during the hours of play in a Test match, couldn't believe their luck. Once the wicket becomes rain-affected it is no longer a contest, and that match provided a major reason why eventually it was decided that wickets should be covered whenever there has been a stoppage.

Denness unfortunately had to suffer and he was a captain about whom my own views had certainly changed. When he first took over at Kent in 1972 I was a little disappointed with his leadership – he was not very flexible and he did not communicate a great deal with his players. Those aspects of his captaincy had improved though by the time we returned from the West Indies in 1974, when he proceeded to do a very good job that summer with England and with Kent. He was always the best one-day captain I played under. He never panicked and he kept very much to set patterns, which certainly helped in limited-overs cricket. Bowlers knew where they were with him because he trusted them to do their job and didn't keep changing them around. You could miss out rather in the one-day game by chopping and changing. Denness loved the limited-overs cricket and really made Kent one of the first counties to appreciate it and to play it as seriously as the three-day matches, which gave us a great advantage. After a hard struggle in his first series as England's captain in the West Indies, he had done so well at home in 1974 that it was very unfortunate for him to have such a difficult series in Australia. Whatever side we had would have struggled against that attack and it would not have mattered who had been captain.

There was another great disappointment for Denness at the end of the 1976 season when, having led the county to the John Player League title and the Benson and Hedges Cup, he lost the captaincy and was replaced by Asif Iqbal. It was an amazing decision; Kent should have stuck with him, because he had improved so much as captain. I was against his going, because he had done such a good job – six trophies won in five years. As is quite often the case, everybody in the Kent camp seemed to know he was being replaced before I did. It was not until the last game of the season at Canterbury, when he asked me to take the team out for the final session of the day, that I realized something might be amiss. There was no reason for me to take over the captaincy, somebody else would normally have done so, but he insisted that I did it. It was a little embarrassing and when I suggested somebody else should lead the side out, he replied, 'I don't want anybody else to take the side out, I want you to do it.' Obviously he knew something was happening; indeed he had been called to attend a meeting in the club's offices. As the dispute between him and the county built up I telephoned him in the early hours one morning to persuade him not to resign.

Denness was succeeded as England captain in the second Test by Tony Greig, whose biggest asset was his great enthusiasm for people. Ironically, because of his epilepsy he had been advised to try and drop off to sleep whenever he could, especially in the late afternoon, but when he was awake he really was a bundle of energy – and one of the most helpful people you could wish to meet. He was always prepared to aid the cause of his players. For example he was responsible for the authorities allowing everyone to have a single room in hotels during Test matches and he also helped tremendously in getting sponsored cars for players. Greig was a cricketer who appealed to the public – he had what is often called charisma. I would say that in recent years Ian Botham has become the Tony Greig of English cricket. Defensively Greig was certainly a better batsman than Botham, who was the better swing bowler at his peak. It is difficult to judge who was the better all-rounder because both had such tremendous all-round performances during their careers. Both were brilliant catchers although Greig held the advantage in this department because his height enabled him to take catches above his head or to dive and take chances which nobody else would get near. What a shame they didn't play together more for England. Greig's enthusiasm and understanding of people ensured that as a captain he was always seeking to get the very best out of his players. He was slightly limited early on in his technical knowledge but he learned very quickly because one of his strong points was that he loved to talk about the game and was prepared to learn (and did so quickly). He had become an excellent captain towards the end of his career, moulding England into a very good side in India in 1976–7. It was a great pity that he never had the chance to develop his captaincy to its full potential.

That series of 1975 saw the emergence on the international scene of Northamptonshire's David Steele, who had always enjoyed the reputation on the county circuit of being a great competitor. He was an ideal person to play under Greig, who liked triers and people who loved the game, and you could not find many better than Steele to slot into that category. In his early days he played forward a great deal with his hands held low, which meant he was either being hit on the gloves or high up on the bat, resulting in chances for the close fielders. So people were worried about his technique at Test level, whether he could play high enough against the quick bowlers and spinners who got plenty of bounce. In Kent we all knew that his batting in this respect had shown a vast improvement because earlier that season he played magnificently on a very bad wicket at Northampton. He had adapted tremendously well, from playing very low to very high, and it came as no surprise to me when he enjoyed a tremendous series. Because of his silver hair he looked older than he was, but in fact he is an extremely youthful man who has kept himself superbly fit. Every moment he is on the pitch excites him and he can't wait to get out and bat. He played very straight, concentrated one hundred per cent, and it was amazing, after his success in 1975 and the following season against the West Indies, that he was left out of the Indian tour in 1976–7. He had played through two hard series at home and then been dropped from a tour which would have suited him ideally. He could bat well against spinners, he could have bowled his left-arm orthodox deliveries, and his close-to-the-wicket catching would have been invaluable. It must have been a great disappointment for somebody who had played so well for his country to have had such a short Test career, yet he never displayed a trace of bitterness – he just carried on enjoying his cricket.

It was fortunate for me that there was no tour in 1975–6 because I was granted a benefit for 1976 (it began in January). It is not a system I favour. For a start it ties a player to the county. He could be there six years before deciding for a variety of reasons that he would welcome a move, but realizing that he could be awarded a benefit in another four years' time he concludes it would not be worth moving. I am not against the idea of players moving from one county to another – a transfer system would not harm cricket. Take soccer for example: spectators are not worried about where the players in their team were born. I don't think cricket fans would be concerned either, and I am sure Kent supporters in 1984 thought of Australian-born Terry Alderman as a Kent player and a very vital one at that. Few of them would have felt he shouldn't have been playing for the county. It would not necessarily mean that the richer counties attracted all the good players. Some soccer clubs pay out tremendous sums of money in transfer fees but don't always get the best teams. It is all a question of the right blend. There are reasons other than money for players wanting to change counties – winter jobs, family reasons, a new challenge or just having been born under a wandering star. It is a shame that if a player wanted to leave a county for family reasons he would

*bove: An awesome sight – Jeff Thomson and Dennis Lillee (right). Lillee was the
*eatest paceman I have seen, and Thommo was a genius for five Tests in 1974–5
*til his shoulder injury in Adelaide, after which he could never bowl quite the same
*ain – a tragedy for cricket.
*ight: Patrick Eagar; left: The Photo Source/Central Press)

*elow: You can see the enthusiastic leadership of Ian Chappell as he shouts
*ngratulations to Dennis Lillee, who has had me caught at second slip by Ian's
*other Greg, one of the finest slip fielders I have ever seen.
*he Photo Source/Central Press)

*Above: Fending off a Thomson bouncer (left) and cutting one high over the slips during that 1974–5 series.    (Patrick Eagar)*

*Below: Doug Walters pulls Bob Willis for 6 off the last ball of the day at Perth, 1974–5, so reaching his century and making 100 runs between tea and the close. Bob went on to become one of England's best-ever fast bowlers.    (Patrick Eagar)*

*Above: Quite a usual sight on past tours if not in England – Bob Taylor keeping wicket, and me at first slip. Mike Hendrick, not a wicket-keeper but one of the safest catchers in the game, is at leg slip.*

*Below right: Bob's certainly got the 'keeping job taped! Concentrating hard, wearing his favourite old gloves.     (Associated Sports Photography)*

*Below left: The old combination – Marsh, b Lillee. A superb leg-side catch ends David Lloyd's innings at Adelaide, 1974–5.*
*(The Photo Source/Central Press)*

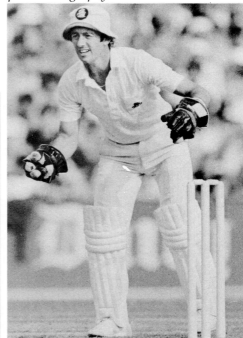

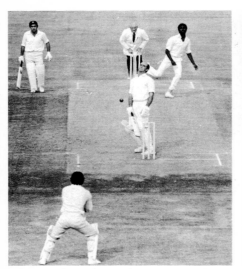
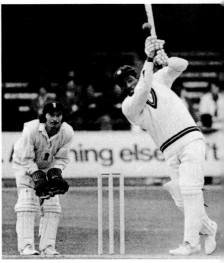

*Above right: What a player! Viv Richards on his way to a double century at Trent Bridge, 1976. Note the tape protecting my broken forefinger.      (Patrick Eagar)*

*Above left: Brian Close is hit by a ball from Michael Holding. John Edrich is batting at the other end. These two veterans faced a bombardment of short-pitched deliveries in this Old Trafford Test. John was a marvellous opening batsman and, although a very strong man, he was short like me, so I studied his game inside out for pointers to help my batting.      (Patrick Eagar)*

*Below: Dropping Wayne Daniel off John Snow at Headingley, 1976. It would have been John's 200th wicket – as I think his expression shows – and the world wicket-keeping record in Tests for me.      (Patrick Eagar)*

*Above: Batting with Tony Greig at Headingley against the West Indies, 1976. Both f us made the same score – 116. It was a very happy day, particularly because the iedia had been suggesting we should both be dropped.     (Patrick Eagar)*

*Below: Stumping Lawrence Rowe at the Oval in 1976 to establish an English vicket-keeping record of 220 victims. It was also a world record at the time. Patrick Eagar)*

*Above: A fantastic catch by Tony Greig, who from second slip has hurled himself in front of Mike Brearley at first slip to take the ball one-handed, during the Centenary Test in Melbourne, 1977. Gary Gilmour was the unlucky batsman.*
*(Patrick Eagar)*

*Below: Derek Randall hooks Lillee for 4 during the same match. Derek went on to score an unforgettable 174.     (Patrick Eagar)*

*Playing the sweep shot during my highest Test innings – 135 against Australia at Trent Bridge in 1977. I shared a stand of 215 with Geoff Boycott (left) in the same match. It was a partnership I shall always remember.*
*(Left: Sport & General; below: Patrick Eagar)*

*Above: Catching Rick McCosker off Tony Greig's bowling . . . and (below) Rod Marsh down the leg-side off Ian Botham at Headingley, 1977. As you can see, the ball only just stayed in my gloves.* (Patrick Eagar)

have to wait five years or so before moving so he could have the chance of being granted a benefit. My feeling is that instead of the benefit system a county should organize fund-raising activities every year and put the money into the wages pot, enabling better salaries to be paid each year which would be much healthier – and give the players some freedom. They would have more money throughout their careers but would not have a benefit towards the end of it.

A benefit year is a very hard one to get through. You find that it is always the same people who tend to support functions which have been organized for you, like golf and cricket matches and dinner dances. That can be embarrassing. You find yourself so occupied that it can be difficult to get your mental approach to the game right and your energy is drained. Godfrey Evans said that in the final Test of 1976 he didn't think my legs were going so well, and I had to agree. If you are going to play cricket regularly throughout the season you cannot afford to have consistent late nights. I kept to a rule about being home by a certain time every evening, which often meant that I left functions early and that again can be embarrassing for those who have helped you. My view was that I had to be fair to myself and to the county, which most people would probably understand. In fact I limited the number of functions that were organized for me during the season.

It might be that a player is unfortunate enough to be injured during his benefit year, which allows him much more time to attend the functions. He could as a result double the size of his benefit, which seems totally unfair on the player who has been a regular member of the side. He might have given tremendous service (and that is surely what the benefit rewards) and played continually throughout his year, but missed out financially by doing so.

A benefit of course is granted by the county. There is no entitlement to it, no qualification, although the general rule is that it may be awarded after a player has been capped for ten years. But for one reason or another a player might have to wait a long time to receive his cap, which can be so hit-and-miss when it is left to the captain. A batsman could really shine in one week, scoring a couple of centuries, and be rewarded with his county cap. He could be unlucky enough to bag a pair and have to wait, perhaps several seasons. John Prodger was capped by Kent on the same day as me, at Dover in 1965, yet he had been on the staff for eleven years longer than I had. He joined the Kent staff in 1952, made his debut four years later, was not capped until 1965 and retired in 1967 – fifteen years' service which was not rewarded by a benefit. There could be a bottleneck as we had in Kent when three players were capped in the 1970 season, when we won the championship. One of them was Bob Woolmer, who only had his benefit in 1984, fourteen years after receiving his cap.

How lucky I was to join Kent when Prodger was on the staff. He was a man who believed in the real joy and happiness of marriage, encouraging me to hold similar thoughts, with the advice: 'Your marriage should always come before your career.' He was best man at my wedding and he and his wife Margaret have remained marvellous friends of ours. Prodger was one of the great catchers, particularly in the slips, where his diving ability was no doubt helped by the fact that he was a goalkeeper who played soccer semi-professionally for Margate and Dartford. I caught the second phase of his batting career. He had opened the innings but then dropped down to the middle order where he became a great attacking batsman against the spinners, particularly because he could take them apart on turning wickets. He had an extraordinarily long stride when playing forward, which helped him to get to the pitch of the ball. He was a very smart, well-turned-out cricketer, a characteristic which never rubbed off on me, but his attitude to the game did: practise and try as hard as possible, but always remember that there are more important things in life than cricket.

My benefit year began on schedule on 1 January 1976, but as the new season approached I began to wonder whether I would play at the start, following a whiplash that developed after I had crashed at Brands Hatch motor-racing circuit. Being a patron of SPARKS, a sportsmen's charity for handicapped children, I had agreed to take part in a charity race and duly attended at the course for a couple of practice sessions. Being a slow, sedate driver with automatic gearbox I was naïve enough to wonder if my automatic Volvo could be my vehicle for the race. The organizers replied that a racing car was necessary – a souped-up Mexico. The instructor drove most of the time on the first practice. It was on the short course but we were reaching speeds of nearly 100 m.p.h. and cornering at no lower than 70 m.p.h. It wasn't long before I had a go myself, in the second practice round. It was a fantastic sensation driving round the track at those speeds and I couldn't wait for race day.

When it came, it was drizzling, and my experience was limited to about one hour's driving of the car and without ever being on a skid patch. On the second circuit of practice, rounding one of the famous bends, I accelerated hard to go downhill and went straight across the road into a barrier. I must have passed out on impact. The next thing I remembered was seeing blood flowing down into my lap and then my head was completely wrapped in bandages. While Jan sat in the stands, waiting for me to appear, I was being taken off to the medical room and then to hospital with a broken nose and facial cuts. What worried the doctors more were the cuts above the eye, one of which was so close that an eye surgeon was called to confirm it was not dangerous. The major problem, however, was my neck, because the crash had given me a whiplash which didn't show up until two days later. We were in our own car when my wife, putting up her arm to adjust my seat-belt, hit me on the nose. My head was thrown back and the whiplash revealed.

My neck has never been the same since. It is such a vital part of your body if you keep wicket and I had to alter my wicket-keeping method considerably. When you stand up straight and bend the top part of your body, with your hips the imaginary hinge, your head is facing down. Then you have to raise the head to see the ball, and that involves the use of the neck muscles which were damaged badly by the whiplash. That's when I struggle. Having my first knock in the pre-season nets I went to protect myself as I hooked a bouncer from Richard Elms and my neck went into a spasm. Then in a pre-season practice match against Sussex Tony Greig (I thought he was my friend!) bowled me a bouncer which I just gloved away only to find my neck going into another spasm as I moved my head quickly back. Fortunately it cleared immediately. On reflection, it's probably not wise for celebrities to go racing round motor tracks without a lot of practice, or without an instructor in the car. John Snow had been involved in a crash at practice a couple of days earlier and it just shows how careful you need to be. I would not recommend it to anyone, although at the time I enjoyed it so much I probably would have taken it up as a hobby.

I had been involved in a car crash in Sydney during the 1974–5 tour which caused a minor whiplash. We were stationary when a car drove straight into the back of us. Again the whiplash was not revealed until a few hours later, by which time we had gone to the beach for a swim and I couldn't lift my head out of the water while swimming on my back. I didn't think that there was any chance of me playing in the Test at Adelaide but Bernard Thomas felt it was worth taking a gamble as it could be better in a day or so. I was glad he gave that advice because it was there that I scored my first century against Australia.

Fortunately the neck problem has not caused quite so much trouble while batting. It has also meant a change in my headgear in recent years because the peak of a cap interfered with my vision when I raised my head when keeping wicket, so I switched to a white floppy hat, the rim of which can be rolled up so that I can see clearly. It was that hat which was reported to the Kent committee a few years ago because members felt it was untidy. For a couple of sessions I wore a new one, but the old one, which had been given to me many years ago in Australia by Fred Titmus, had proved ideal. It was just the right weight and I was reluctant to throw it out – a stand on which I was supported by some Kent members who were prepared to petition the committee on my behalf. A compromise solution was found – the wife of one of the Kent officials, Chris Taylor, got busy with her needle and repaired the offending hat, which I have worn ever since.

For the first Test of the 1976 series against the West Indies at Trent Bridge, it was touch and go whether I was fit enough to play, having broken my finger batting against Wayne Daniel for Kent at Canterbury. I remember I had played on until tea and then after the interval the spinner Albert Padmore came on and I whacked the first ball up into the air. I was deliberately trying to get out because I was in so much pain, but it was a no-ball. I had to retire hurt and some of the press reported that I had broken the finger against Padmore. I was not altogether certain that I would be fit for the Test match, but eventually I played. Roger Tolchard had been called up as replacement wicket-keeper instead of Bob Taylor, presumably because of Tolchard's superior batting. The match itself ended in a draw, Vivian Richards of course made a double century, and the game was also notable for David Steele's maiden Test century.

The second Test at Lord's also ended in a draw when the West Indies were 241 for 6 in their second innings, needing 323 to win. England lost the third Test at Old Trafford by 425 runs. It was the occasion when Brian Close and John Edrich opened the batting and were given a terrible roasting by the West Indies' fast bowlers on the Saturday evening of the match. I can remember that as early as the first over of the day, when a ball flew from Mike Selvey who had been drafted in for the game because all the leading English opening bowlers were injured, we all looked at each other and thought what a bad wicket it was going to be. Batting fourth we knew that we might have difficulties, and so it turned out. England were bowled out for 71 and 126.

The fourth Test match at Headingley really was a great match, the West Indies winning by 55 runs. After Old Trafford there were rumours that there might be some changes in the team, including Tony Greig and myself, so it was satisfying for us both that we managed to make runs at Headingley. It is the nicest time to go and get runs when you feel that there is talk of your being dropped. England actually had a great chance to win the match but were bowled out for 204 by Roberts, Holding and Daniel, who bowled particularly fast. Greig again made runs in the second innings and finished unbeaten on 76, but I recall that the loss of Peter Willey on the penultimate evening was particularly crucial to our cause.

The fifth Test match at the Oval was my seventy-eighth for England. I managed to break Godfrey Evans's Test record of 219 dismissals when I stumped Lawrence Rowe for 70 (fittingly off my old partner for Kent and England, Derek Underwood). I do remember, though, that I might have broken the record earlier at Headingley by taking a catch off John Snow, which would also have been his 200th Test wicket, but I dropped a dolly. Godfrey Evans, after I had broken the record, sent some champagne up to the dressing room. The match of course will be remembered not for Alan Knott breaking the record for wicket-keeping dismissals in Test matches, but for a great spell of bowling by Michael Holding. He finished the game with 14 wickets for 149 runs, taking 8 in the first innings and 6 in the second. He bowled quicker through the air in that match at the Oval than I have ever

seen anybody bowl. He was certainly as quick through the air as
Jeff Thomson had been in 1974–5, but Thommo always had that
devastating pace and bounce off the wicket.

When the time came to consider my availability for the tour to
India in 1976–7 followed by the Centenary Test against Australia
in Melbourne there were two problems – family and my own
physical condition. After the illness I suffered during the 1972–3
tour I had to consider that aspect very carefully. I eventually
decided to go mainly because Tony Greig was captain and
because Jan was allowed to join me on the tour at the time we had
requested. Before we went I looked very carefully into what my
eating and drinking habits should be on the trip, seeking the
advice of Bob Woolmer's mother, who had lived in India. She
provided a list of 'dos and don'ts' for European tummies – food
has to be very well cooked; only eat fruit that you can peel; eat
eggs, and toast with the crusts off; eat nothing that has been
washed and put no ice in your drinks. Those were some of the
useful points she made. I stuck absolutely rigidly to her instructions and I was so relieved not to have any problems. The water is
the main difficulty but fortunately on that 1976–7 tour there was a
special bottled water, which was ideal. You could even clean your
teeth with it, which was preferable to the Scotch and soda water I
had used previously.

England had a superb series against India in the event. We won
the first three Tests. The first was at Delhi, where John Lever of
Essex made his Test debut. He not only took 7 wickets in an
innings for 53 runs, but also scored a maiden Test half-century.
We won the second Test by ten wickets, Tony Greig making an
absolutely brilliant century and Roger Tolchard, in his Test debut
(as a batsman only), an invaluable 67. Bob Willis also proved his
worth in that series and it was then that I felt he started to become
a really good opening Test bowler. He started to bowl line and
length consistently and pretty quickly. At Madras in the third
Test Bishen Bedi, the great Indian left-arm spinner, became the
first Indian to take 200 wickets in Test matches, but England won
by 200 runs to secure the series. The wicket also suited our seam
bowlers and John Lever took five wickets in the first innings with
Bob Willis taking three in the second to finish the match, as India
were bowled out very cheaply indeed second time round, for 83.
India won the fourth Test and we nearly lost the final match of the

series. I remember that Karsan Ghavri, the opening seam bowler, came on with spinners, took five wickets and had us in a little bit of bother. In the end we held on for a draw.

Next it was on to Australia for their Centenary Test. Of course it was an occasion that one will always remember. Nobody could have expected the result to be identical to that of the first Test between England and Australia a hundred years before. Derek Randall's second innings of 174 has become legend, of course. It was a really brilliant innings. He just took the attack to the bowlers and when Tony Greig and I were together on the last afternoon we sensed at one point that England could win the match, but when Greig was out we felt the pressure a little bit. I knew the need to keep making runs and to make sure I got the strike. In the event I was the last man out when I was l.b.w. to Lillee for 42 and England were dismissed for 417. It was an unusual match in that you knew that it was just a one-off affair. You knew that if you lost you didn't have four matches in the series to go, so to that extent it was relaxing but, of course, it was a match both sides wanted to win. Playing for a draw, which we could have done, would have been pointless. Greig's instructions were to go for victory at all costs.

Derek Randall deservedly won the Man of the Match award, which was a shame for Rodney Marsh, who must have had the greatest possible game for a wicket-keeper/batsman. During the match he broke the record for victims by an Australian 'keeper in Test cricket. When he broke my world record at Headingley in 1981, I sent him some champagne, with a card saying, 'Well done, hope you don't drop the bottle.' I was glad it was him who broke my record, because he was such a fantastic cricketer. As a 'keeper the great strength in his legs enabled him to make so much ground when standing back, and up to the wicket he was the fastest stumper I have seen. It was his competitive attitude which resulted in his taking some amazing reaction catches, stood up, making so much ground for wide deflections when standing back or sprinting long distances after the steepling skyer. In World Series Cricket he took one of the greatest catches I've seen – chasing a skyer, overrunning it and then diving back, parallel to the ground, about three feet above it, catching the ball with arms at full stretch. How he held on to it when he hit the ground I cannot imagine. Mentally and physically he was tremendously fit. If he missed a simple chance he just kept going as if nothing had happened. He seemed to love the big occasion, giving every ounce of energy and concentration.

His appearance could have been misleading to the public because he never smiled much on the pitch, hunched his shoulders, clasped his hands behind his back and had a loud, vigorous appeal, which might not have gone down too well with English fans. His very competitive approach hid his warm personality – and Derek Randall had reason to appreciate that when he played his magnificent innings in the Centenary Test at Melbourne. For Randall, edging Greg Chappell, was given out caught behind on 161, but Marsh immediately called him back as he walked, intimating that the ball hadn't carried, a fact that we had not appreciated from the pavilion. Apparently Greg Chappell had remarked to Marsh, 'Have you gone all religious?'

At Perth during the 1970–1 tour I was involved in two appeals with Marsh while batting against Keith Stackpole, bowling his leg-spinners. England were up against it and I hadn't scored when I swept at a ball. It went on to my gloves, over Marsh's head and was caught at slip. The umpire gave me 'not out' and there were a few remarks passed. Stackpole subsequently switched ends and again I swept, again I gloved the ball, and Marsh took the catch. He wasn't sure what the ball had hit as Stackpole went up, appealing, but again the verdict was 'not out'. Meanwhile Marsh looked at me and said, 'Did you hit it?' but I didn't reply. What are you meant to say in a situation like that? If I had said 'yes' Marsh would have appealed. At Test level I have always felt you are encouraged not to walk. If one side walks and the other doesn't, it could be a very unfair contest. There were no set instructions; players just made their own decision, but captains at Test level generally preferred you not to walk.

In county cricket I would always walk and I would think about 66 per cent of the players do, but all the same it is getting less common. I remember Les Ames telling me that in the old days nobody walked at all, and he thought that this was a much happier arrangement. It was left to the umpire who, after all, is there to make the decisions.

Marsh was involved in one of the most unusual sights I have ever seen on a cricket field. During World Series Cricket he had borrowed a helmet from Dennis Amiss. During his innings he was hit on the head and when he suddenly remembered that he was wearing a helmet he almost yelled out with relief and there was joy all over his face.

In the 1970–1 series he was cruelly dubbed 'Iron Gloves', but by the end of his career he had become a legend in his time, and certainly one of my all-time heroes.

# Ten

# Packer

Packer – a name that was to have such an impact on the cricket world. It was to stir passions at every level of the game as the arguments for and against raged – from the cricket boards of individual countries down through English county cricket clubs and their members, and to the players themselves who eventually voted by 91 to 77 to ban from playing those of their colleagues who signed for World Series Cricket. The first time I heard the name was in the telephone conversation with Tony Greig in March 1977 which I have described in Chapter 1. Greig had certainly got something to interest me when he mentioned that the plan included cricket in Australia during the winter with no restriction on wives and families. Not many details were revealed in that phone call. The original scheme was for a World team to play Australia, and England, the West Indies, Pakistan and South Africa would be involved. Greig trusted me not to say anything about our conversation. It was the day before I was due in London to take part in his 'This is Your Life' programme, so I wasn't able to mention that we would be meeting the next day. It was a strange coincidence that during that period Greig and I were closely involved other than in the Packer plans. Kent had pre-season friendlies with Sussex and we also attended, on 20 April in London, the dinner at which I was presented with the

Walter Lawrence Trophy for hitting the fastest century of the 1976 season – ironically against Sussex at Canterbury. Greig had to introduce me as the winner in front of many of cricket's hierarchy, including members of the Test and County Cricket Board. Like me, Greig wondered what those people would think when they knew what had gone on.

There had been a meeting in London involving half a dozen players at which more information was made available. I already believed in the concept of World Series Cricket – it answered my own personal requirements and could help to change and develop the game, which I believed necessary. It seemed to me that the administrators were extremely slow to consider changes in the game which would benefit those involved. The plan for World Series Cricket (WSC) was to play during the winter months on reasonably short tours. The guarantee that my family could be with me was a major factor in influencing my support. There were to be no restrictions – families could travel by the same transport as the players instead of using separate flights as was the policy on the MCC tour to Australia in 1974–5. When I went on an England tour and Jan came with me I would just about break even, whereas with WSC I would show a profit. By signing, however, Greig might miss out on promotional activities, resulting in a decrease in his overall earnings in this country. So financially there might not be such a tremendous advantage in him joining.

However, I also believed that players should be more in the minds of the administrators, who gave the impression that they believed cricketers would always play because they loved the game so much. The advent of WSC meant that suddenly there was a second employer in the game, which must be healthy in this case. One lot of ideas should bounce off the other and both sets of administrators would be pushing each other higher. It was nice for players to have a choice. I liked the idea of playing in the best available standard of cricket, which I thought WSC would be – as indeed it was. There was never a match when you weren't playing against top international opposition. I did consider how WSC could affect my England career, but after the problems I had encountered over touring I felt my Test career abroad could anyway be over. It was always clear that my availability for England in home series would not be jeopardized, if I were selected. Kerry Packer, contrary to many people's ideas, never wanted to see Test cricket discontinued.

The news about WSC broke in England on Monday, 9 May, and the hostile reaction in the press surprised me. I had not expected that because I had reckoned that most people would agree with my view that it was very healthy to have two employers in the game. On the Wednesday of that week Kent began a three-day championship match with Middlesex at Lord's during which Asif Iqbal, Derek Underwood and myself had a meeting with the then county chairman, Walter Brice, to discuss the matter. All I really remember from that meeting was Mr Brice expressing the view that our commitment to WSC made no difference to Kent. Underwood and I also met the TCCB's Donald Carr and Doug Insole at Lord's. They were basically just trying to discover what WSC was all about and at that stage we were not very sure of the detailed plans ourselves. I recall Mr Insole saying in reference to Packer, 'Does he need a manager?'

Some people seemed to resent the way in which those of us who had agreed to sign had acted so secretively. Greig seemed to take the main blast of that accusation but I didn't feel at all guilty and nor should he have done. It had to be secret because if the news had emerged the authorities would have tried to quash the plans before they were really in motion. Sure enough, that is what happened when the news did emerge.

Packer was not trying to threaten Test cricket – his immediate plans just clashed with the England tour to Pakistan and New Zealand and the Indian trip to Australia. He had to start somewhere and the original plan for the winter of 1977–8 was to play specially arranged matches, beginning with a series of six five-day Tests, six one-day games, and six three-day round robin tournaments. In my view Packer was driven into a corner when his players were banned and he therefore had to revise his plans. We knew before we signed that we would not be available for the England tour. Yet many players in the past had missed out on tours under different circumstances but had still returned to play for England. It had been quite acceptable; indeed Alec Bedser, then chairman of the selectors, had never toured anywhere apart from Australia and New Zealand, and once to South Africa. I can't believe that if he had been available he would not have been picked.

I felt sorry for Tony Greig when he was sacked as the England captain. He genuinely believed that WSC would be very good for the game, and he put that before his position as England skipper. People alleged that he had signed for financial reasons but he was already an exceptionally well-off cricketer in England as the personality player of the era. If they were going to fight WSC, the administrators had no option but to sack him. Ray Illingworth hadn't gone to India in 1972–3 yet he had taken over the captaincy again from Tony Lewis after that tour. It was different in Greig's case, in so far as he was going off to play in another form of cricket. His dismissal was disappointing for another reason: he had become a very good captain and England a very good team. Fortunately during the 1976–7 tour Greig and his vice-captain Mike Brearley had worked together extremely well and this successful partnership continued after Brearley had been appointed as Greig's successor. Brearley made it quite clear to the players that he was only captain because of the advent of WSC and he stressed that it was Greig who had built up such a good side. Throughout the series with Australia in the summer of 1977 the atmosphere was perfect in the England dressing room, and the credit for that goes to Brearley and Greig.

Occasionally selectors would question those of us involved in WSC, particularly towards the end of the summer, about whether we might change our minds. It was all done in a very friendly way and I was asked the question at Headingley during the fourth Test by Charlie Elliott. My answer was that I would not be changing my mind. After the second Test at Old Trafford Dennis Amiss was dropped, which seemed a very harsh decision. He had enjoyed such a fantastic series in India that I wondered whether he would have been left out if he had not signed for WSC.

The continued hostility in the media never worried me because I hardly ever read it. One of the best pieces of advice ever given to me came from former Australian Test cricketer Keith Miller at a dinner in the West Indies in 1968. By then following a new career as a cricket writer, Miller advised me to try not to read or listen to the media. The problem is that especially when you are a senior player colleagues keep asking if you have read what someone has written in the newspapers. I have never read them much anyway, because I am not a great reader. When playing Test cricket there is normally a television on in the dressing room but most captains have a rule that the sound is turned down. It's a good idea because a commentator might make a remark about a player which would upset him and the rest of the side. The only time I really watch cricket on the television is to study technique, particularly of bowlers against whom I'll be batting and bowlers to whom I'll be keeping wicket.

Throughout the summer of 1977 I encountered only one personal instance of hostility – at Chesterfield. Because of my rivalry with Bob Taylor for the England wicket-keeping job, the Derbyshire fans had never given me a very warm reception. On this particular Sunday a chap grabbed hold of me, started shaking me and said, 'How are you worth all that money?' I had to interrupt him, saying, 'Sorry, I'm on my way out to bat.' When I reached the middle some of the crowd really roared their disapproval. I hit Mike Hendrick for what I thought would be a certain six, but the fielder on the fence, Fred Swarbrook, leaned backwards and caught the ball. The crowd really loved that but Kent had the final word, because we won the match off the last ball.

At Derby, where we played the championship game, I was amused when a man called John Cornell turned up. He was quite an important person in the Packer set-up but no one on the ground had any idea who he was. Seen from the players' box he looked on that day an unobtrusive spectator, but his mission in Derby was to talk to my Kent colleague and West Indian Test cricketer Bernard Julien about WSC.

Strangely enough, during that series I hardly discussed WSC with Geoff Boycott. He made a reference to it during the final Test at the Oval, when he said how much he had enjoyed playing cricket with me over the years but felt that life was now going to see us following separate routes. He seemed to know what sort of division was to come in the game and he probably appreciated more than I did the possible consequences.

It was during that Test that Bob Woolmer was approached about signing for Packer. I was in Greig's room on the night Bob came to discuss the matter. He was offered terms and eventually signed. Because he knew that Bob and I were good friends Greig had asked me to be there. Before I could leave his room following the chat with Woolmer another Bob arrived – Willis. Greig discussed with him for about twenty minutes the prospects of his joining WSC. Willis left and in the event he didn't join Packer, although he might have come very close to doing so.

Meanwhile I was happy with my decision and wasn't persuaded to change my mind by the efforts of businessman David Evans to bring more money into the game, particularly at Test level. It merely supported the argument that WSC would have an overall benefit on cricket and that more money would be forthcoming for the game. In the past we could have been paid, as England players, for wearing the emblem of a certain firm in one-day internationals but the authorities would not allow it. It provoked talk in the England dressing room of a players' strike, which never materialized, but it confirmed my view that administrators felt players would always turn out even if they were really struggling to make a living. Most administrators from county level upwards do their jobs in an honorary capacity, having other income; I'm not sure they appreciated that cricket wages were low or on the other hand how difficult it was to survive on such low pay. But WSC was going to bring more money into the game. That would encourage young sportsmen to go into cricket who might have decided to play a game that was more lucrative or not play professional sport at all. Before the fourth Test, when Brearley was handed a cheque for £9000 by Evans, some people suggested that the Packer players in the England side should not get a share. Brearley made it clear that we were a team and every member would receive his share. I have always strongly believed that all bonuses should be split amongst the whole squad.

On 10 August it was announced by the TCCB that Packer players would be banned from taking part in county cricket. We had received legal advice that this could not be enforced; and I had made my decision to join Packer and was going to stand by it. It did amaze me, though, when the county players subsequently voted in favour of the ban, because I felt that WSC was going to do a lot for the game financially and that the county players would have been in agreement, because in addition their own status would have been improved. Certainly the wages of Kent approximately doubled in the season following WSC and umpires' fees were considerably boosted, especially at Test level. One umpire even asked me to thank Packer for his rise! More than the purely financial benefits, I felt that WSC had created an atmosphere where players were enabled to air their views and indeed have them taken seriously – a question of improving the standing of the player and his position in the game. I can only repeat that it was a direct consequence of having two employers where before there had been only one.

I gave evidence at the High Court hearing in which declarations were sought that all the recommendations of the International Cricket Conference were an unreasonable restraint of trade. It began on 27 September and on 28 November judgement was given in favour of the three cricketers who had brought the action – Tony Greig, Mike Procter and John Snow.

I remember regretting that I had declined the opportunity to sit while giving my evidence, not realizing that I would be in the witness box for two hours. I think everyone knew what the result of the case would be. It surprised me that it ever came to court, because everybody seemed to think that the TCCB had no chance of winning. I had decided that if by any chance I was not allowed to play county cricket it would of course be a shame but I would just have to play WSC and I was looking forward very much to the first season during the winter of 1977–8.

I was astonished by the small crowds at the start of WSC but it certainly grew in popularity and proved to be the most competitive cricket in which I have played. It was hard because the standard was so high with all the talent around. There were rumours that some of the games were fixed, which was absolutely ridiculous because the players had so much pride at stake and the Aussies in particular were desperate to win because they were playing in front of their own crowds. The WSC Australian side was the major draw, particularly in the second year, because their Test side was again very weak. The Test team had got away with it in the first year against India but in the second year England provided much better opposition and beat them 5–1. By that second year there was no doubt that the Australian public was following WSC.

Another suggestion, which I dispute, was that some of the aggravation between Tony Greig and Ian Chappell, the respective captains, was contrived. In the past they seemed to have had a great respect for each other, though it did not stop them having a go at one another. By WSC, however, that respect seemed to have disappeared, especially from Chappell towards Greig.

There was a very genuine confrontation at Perth when Greig, who was in poor form with the bat, went out to run for Gordon Greenidge, who had a leg injury. Greig wasn't wearing a helmet, which he usually did when batting, so Chappell immediately complained that he should have been wearing one. Rodney Marsh made a humorous but friendly remark that Greig wasn't wearing a helmet because it was at the panel-beater's – a reference to the fact that Greig had been hit on the head earlier during his innings. Eventually Chappell said, 'Oh well, let him do it. He's never out here long enough when he bats.' Chappell may also have taken exception to the fact that the captain had come out to run and could pass on instructions. Then at the end of the Super Test when the World had beaten Australia, Chappell shook Greig's hand and sarcastically said, 'Another great hand from you!', Greig having got a low score again.

Greig was by no means alone in being struck while batting. Many players were hit as a result of bowling which was very, very fast. No one held back the bouncers – numbers nine, ten and eleven got their full share too on the basis that if they were fast bowlers delivering bouncers themselves they would have to receive them in turn. The fast bowlers of yesteryear pitched the ball up to each other. That was not the practice in WSC. I remember Dennis Lillee bouncing Joel Garner, because that was the treatment he himself had received from the big West Indian pacemen. The bowling was so quick and of such a high standard that even the great Viv Richards was struck on the head, and that's a sight I've only seen in WSC. It was easy to understand the situation when you glanced at the fast-bowling line-up: Australia – Lillee, Pascoe; World – Imran Khan, Le Roux, Rice, Procter; West Indies – Holding, Croft, Daniel, Garner and Roberts. The pace bowling on the Sydney Show Ground in the one-day final was lethal. When I had played there earlier in the series it was the fastest wicket I had ever experienced. It was a true wicket but very quick and bouncy. To Garner I was standing further back than I had ever been in my career. In that match I remember Greg Chappell gloving a ball from Andy Roberts off his face. It was one of the fastest deliveries I have seen and his colour just drained. The next ball bowled him. It was easy to understand why helmets were used in WSC, introduced by Dennis Amiss, whose helmet was like a motorcyclist's. When he walked out to bat the crowd shouted, 'Hey, Amiss, you've forgotten your bike.' I had tried it but was dubious about viewing through perspex. I remember at Adelaide the first ball I received from Michael Holding I got an inside edge; the next Tony Greig called for a run and I didn't hear him properly. I set off, then he shouted 'No'; I didn't hear that clearly either and when I tried to get back I was run out by yards.

One of the big successes in WSC was the use of the white ball. It's a must for spectators, who could see it so much better, by day or night. I must have been some 200 yards from the bat at Perth, on my way to the nets, when Dennis Amiss edged Andy Roberts to be caught at slip. It was like watching cricket in slow motion. With the red ball a spectator is often unsure exactly what happened – has the player missed it, struck it for four or been caught? One of the problems with the white ball was that the white was not impregnated in the leather so that the top coat could come off. This resulted in the only farcical situation in WSC. In a Super Test at Melbourne, during a night session, Imran Khan was bowling brilliantly for the World, making the ball swing all over the place, and naturally desperate to retain the shine on the ball. Because the white substance which was used on the ball tended to come off it could be recoated, which removed the shine. The batsman kept asking the umpire for the ball to be recoated. When his request was granted all our players were immediately trying to rub it off as quickly as possible so that the ball would start swinging again. Very interesting but very unusual cricket tactics. In the end Imran won the day, continuing to swing the ball very late.

If you use the white ball, you have to have coloured clothing (another WSC innovation) otherwise it is hard to see the ball against the background of white pads or flannels. It was a difficulty I quickly appreciated as a wicket-keeper. The best example of the problem it could cause came when the ball was driven into the covers where the fielder Asif couldn't pick it out against the white background of the batsman. It struck him on the body while he was still trying to sight it. Anyway, in this modern, fashion-conscious world coloured clothing must be a great attraction. It could well bring much more money into the game because youngsters are more likely to buy a coloured shirt for casual wear than an ordinary white one.

The atmosphere of night cricket was much better than by day, and probably the same is true of soccer in this country under floodlights. You tend to get a bigger crowd because people come straight from work. The lights at Sydney were so good that it was like playing in daylight, but at VFL Park, Melbourne, they were not so good, although they were adequate under normal conditions. In that Super Test at Melbourne, on a very misty evening, the ball swung around and one ball from Imran Khan seemed to swing almost at right angles, bowling Rodney Marsh as he padded up. The great advantage of night cricket in Australia, especially in the heatwave of that summer, was that it avoided the necessity of playing in a temperature of 90 degrees plus, with high humidity, during the day. It was much better to play in the cool of the evening.

Night cricket was a great idea and it might be feasible in England, although heavy dews could cause problems, making day and night conditions very different and forcing sides to adapt accordingly. In the evening, with the outfield soaked by the dew, the wet ball could become soft and lose its shine, making bowling and fielding much harder in the night session than in the day. It could be argued that conditions can always change during a match. Provided the dew was not troublesome, night cricket would surely be a great attraction in England. To be practicable for county cricket, it would have to be successful in London and the other big cities, where people could finish their day's work and go straight off to watch the game. With their employment unaffected it would bring in more people to watch championship or even Test cricket. It could be a wise move to experiment with night cricket in English conditions as soon as possible, installing floodlights on the big grounds, to ascertain whether cricket could follow the success of evening soccer, rugby and athletics. It would be nice to see a repeat of the scene at Sydney for its first floodlit match. The public seats were crammed to capacity with so many people trying to get in. Admittedly, the small members' enclosure was nearly empty – a sign of reaction perhaps.

Night cricket meant adapting to new working hours. Instead of a lunch interval, because play started then, there was one for dinner, an hour's break with a big three-course meal available for those who wanted it. There was also the hazard one night of the cicadas, who were disturbed by the lights. They emerged to show their disapproval, flying around overhead in the same way, no doubt, as the pigeons at the Oval would react to night cricket. It was an odd feeling to finish play for the day at 10.30 p.m. Having rarely eaten dinner during the interval I was usually hungry. So I would normally have a meal around midnight, unwind by watching the late-night movie and get to bed about 2 a.m. The seven-and-a-half-hour day was very arduous. It was too long and meant that there was always the possibility of players getting tired, losing their ability slightly, and so possibly reducing the high standards. On one occasion, the West Indies, playing against the World, had to field for the entire seven and a half hours. Moreover, their wicket-keeper Deryck Murray was injured and Desmond Haynes found himself behind the stumps for the whole day. It was the first time he had kept for many years and unfortunately things didn't go well for him. Being in the field for that length of time is obviously harder on the wicket-keeper than anyone else, because bowlers at least have the chance of a break between their overs and their spells. I know that Haynes suffered the next day with sore and badly bruised hands.

There was no doubt that to play these extended hours players had to be super fit and that is another direction in which WSC has been of benefit to Test cricket. Not only has international cricket become far more competitive, Test sides have also followed the example of WSC teams in concentrating on fitness. Although Bernard Thomas always worked very hard on fitness in the England camp I was never quite sure how fit some of the other Test sides were. But they have all seemed far fitter since. In that second year of WSC I was convinced that it had become so good for the game that any youngster starting out on a cricket career, even the young professionals already in the game, would benefit from watching it. Even television coverage has been transformed since WSC with the number of cameras, the slow-motion replays from different angles, the replays of most wicket falls from the bowler's end and a split screen allowing the viewer to watch batsman and fielder.

One of my main reasons for joining WSC was to sample cricket of the highest possible standard and I was not disappointed. Barry Richards facing Dennis Lillee at the top level was something I had always wanted to see, a sight which cricket followers all over the world would have welcomed. A great confrontation came in the second season of WSC, during the final Super Test, which was one of the most exciting cricket matches in which I have ever played. It was Australia against the World, with both teams absolutely at peak form. It was Richards's game because in the last innings, on a wicket that was not very good for the batsman, he steered the World home to victory with a magnificent unbeaten century.

To have my wife Jan and my son James with me throughout the two years of WSC was wonderful – and that really had been my major reason for signing. Everything was laid on for wives and children, which removed any pressure from the players. WSC was based in Melbourne for the first winter and in Sydney for the second, with good accommodation and offices always available to deal with any family problems. Many of the players had their families with them; there were always special rooms for them at the grounds; and the whole set-up represented a different world for me from that which had existed on England tours.

The end of WSC and my touring days with England have meant missing out on playing in Australia, particularly at Sydney, my favourite ground of all, and on playing against that great foursome Dennis Lillee, Rod Marsh, Ian Chappell and Greg Chappell. Ian Chappell was the best captain I played against at Test level; there was always a big difference when he led the side. His players respected him greatly and he really got them buzzing. He was great talking to his bowlers, who never seemed to have quite the same competitive attitude if he wasn't skipper. He never had a go at anyone verbally when leading his side in the field, which is a good thing because if you lose control of yourself you are quick to respond in very aggressive and strong language.

Derek Underwood, for example, would exclaim 'Ah!' in frustration, and Chappell would moan back at him to try and stir him up. Yes, he might well swear, needing to do so to gee himself up. We never minded because we felt he didn't play so well when he was in this mood; when he was quieter he was a much more dangerous and secure batsman. Later in his career, Chappell generally never talked to you on the pitch. If you said, 'Well played!' when he got 50 or 100 he just wouldn't answer. The Aussies seemed to have this plan under the second stage of his captaincy. I used to say 'Hello' in the middle to Rodney Marsh, for instance, but in one match he didn't want to answer, obviously because he had been told not to. When I scored my first century against Australia – in Adelaide on the 1974–5 tour – he did shake my hand and congratulate me, which made the moment all the more thrilling. The only conversation Ian Chappell would indulge in was if somebody else was having a go at him, and then he would reply. His attitude made him a tremendous player – he fought all the time and the harder the conditions and the worse the match was going, the better he seemed able to play. During the 1970–1 tour it seemed certain he would lose his place in Melbourne. He was dropped two or three times but battled on and reached a century. That is when he was at his best – when the chips were down. He had a very unusual technique against quick bowling, which paid off for him. He used to get right back with his pads in front of the stumps and played with his bat in front of his legs, just as if it were French cricket. Technically, he was not such a good player as his younger brother Greg, who was one of the best batsmen I have ever seen. Greg played tremendously straight. He kept very still and played high, and that made him very good against quick bowlers.

# *Eleven*
# County and Test Recall

When I returned to England in March 1978, having taken a holiday in Sydney and California at the end of the WSC season, there was no doubt that my future in county cricket was in jeopardy. It was made very clear at a meeting that my solicitor and I had with members of the Kent committee that the committee would prefer me not to play. The county had decided that they would offer only one-year contracts, which would not be renewed, to their four Packer players – Asif Iqbal, Derek Underwood, Bob Woolmer and myself – an attitude that surprised me. When I asked the chairman, John Pocock, what the committee would really like me to do he said they would prefer me not to play. I could see Kent's position: it would be my last season, having only been offered a one-year contract and they had in Paul Downton a young wicket-keeper who had already been on an England tour. So I could appreciate that even if I took the one-year contract I might not be playing much. As the people employing me didn't really want me to play it could result in a very awkward atmosphere. After a meeting before the season started, when both sides had their solicitors present, the following statement was issued jointly by the club and myself:

> The Kent County Cricket Club recently announced that it would be offering one-year Contracts only to each of the four

Kent players who are contracted to play World Series Cricket.
The Committee subsequently announced that those Contracts
would not be renewed after the 1978 season.

It is against that background and the fact that the Club
naturally wishes to give every opportunity to its younger
players and in particular to Paul Downton that the Club and
Alan Knott have discussed his future.

It was mutually agreed that it would be in the interests of
Kent cricket that Alan Knott should not play for the County
during the 1978 season.

The Club and player are parting on extremely amicable
terms and Alan Knott has agreed that his registration as a
County Cricketer shall remain with Kent for the 1978 season.

So I went off and worked in my sports shop at Herne Bay and
hardly missed cricket. What helped to a certain extent was that
during the season I was engaged in doing some commentating
for television, which provided an occasional chance to see the
lads, but otherwise I never went to cricket. I knew that I would be
playing again in the winter with WSC, so it was not as though it
was the end of my career. I wondered whether the pre-season
atmosphere would have meant that I wouldn't have enjoyed
my cricket if I had played. Although the committee had their
thoughts on the matter, I knew that the new captain Alan Ealham
had wanted me to play. Ealham had taken over from Asif and I
wished him all the best for the season – he is one of the nicest
people you could meet in the game. It had seemed a harsh
decision by Kent to sack Asif from the captaincy. Although I had
felt he should not have been skipper and that Mike Denness
should have continued in that role, Asif proved himself to be a
very fine leader. Still, Ealham had great success in his first
season, leading Kent to the county championship title and to the
Benson and Hedges Cup, and I was delighted for him.

Towards the end of the season Arthur Phebey, a former Kent
batsman and the then chairman of the cricket sub-committee,
came to see me, after Downton had decided that he would be
returning to university to continue his studies for a law degree.
By now Kent had changed their mind about the future of their
Packer players and announced that they would be offering them
new contracts. So they wanted me to play again and suggested
that I should be engaged for the first half of the 1979 and 1980

seasons to cover the time when Downton would be at university and therefore unavailable to play for them, and I agreed.

My playing career in 1978 resumed in strange surroundings – in the Shea Stadium in New York, playing for the Rest of the World against an American All-Stars XI. Despite the lack of publicity because of a newspaper strike there was still a crowd of around 13,000 to see the American side, composed mainly of West Indian cricketers living in the States, take on some of the best-known cricketing names in the world. Our side included Barry Richards, David Hookes, Greg Chappell, Tony Greig, Andy Roberts, Gary Sobers and Bishen Bedi. It was a great pleasure to keep wicket to Bishen, one of the great left-arm spinners of all time, and it was a thrill to take a catch off his bowling. On an unusual wicket – matting placed on top of the diamond cinders, which produced an uneven bounce – we were badly beaten but it was a good experience, playing in one of the world's most famous baseball stadiums, and I felt that cricket could definitely go well in America, particularly in New York.

My second season with WSC in 1978–9 was even more enjoyable than the first, which made it so disappointing for me when it was announced, just before the start of the 1979 season in England, that it was all over.

The Australian Cricket Board signed an agreement with PBL Sports Ltd, one of Kerry Packer's subsidiaries, giving PBL exclusive television rights in Australian cricket for ten years. Television rights, of course, had been associated with Packer's original decision to form WSC. Under the agreement, the Board also agreed to consider favourably fielding circles, day–night cricket and coloured clothing – all of them now, of course, commonplace features of Australian cricket. The International Cricket Conference approved the agreement between the Australian board and Packer at its annual meeting later in 1979.

It was a great surprise that the end had come; only a couple of days earlier, at a Players' Association meeting, I had been extolling its merits. It had provided such a high standard of cricket, had got over most of its teething problems and had confirmed my view that two employers was healthy for the game. More jobs had been provided, more people had become involved with the game. More players had a chance at the top level; young sportsmen were encouraged to think more towards cricket; there was increased financial security.

I played during the first half of 1979 for Kent, as had been agreed, but declined to carry on for the rest of the season, which they suddenly wanted me to do. I had made other arrangements for my business and for holidays, so I decided to stick to the contract that had been made. Kent's mood had changed about my future, because apart from being very keen for me to play for the whole season, they later approached me about playing full time again. It might have been because other counties had been expressing an interest in my future and because there had been some talk about my going to Australia on England's winter tour of 1979–80. By then I was feeling that I might want to play again on a more permanent basis because there had been interest shown by other counties, some serious, others on a more casual basis. I went to see the chairman of one county and there had been approaches of a more tentative nature by two county captains, who had often talked to me about moving. In one case I had asked the captain concerned whether, if I moved, it could be as a batsman only, but it didn't suit him. My dream had always been to play for England purely as a batsman.

Moving to another county would involve many considerations, the most important being my business and moving house. I must admit to having been reasonably interested in offers I had of two-year contracts, one of which was from Nottinghamshire. Interest had also been expressed by three other counties. The problem was that I was playing for Kent for the first half of 1979 and had contracted to do so again in 1980, which meant investigating whether I would be able to swop counties midway through the 1980 season after Downton's return from university to play for Kent. Kent's wish that I should sign a lengthy contract surprised me, because Downton had been keeping well. Eventually there was a meeting at the house of the chairman John Pocock, attended by the cricket sub-committee chairman Arthur Phebey, where they talked in terms of a four-year contract. Eventually that was the contract offered to both Downton and me – I accepted but Paul, quite understandably after Kent had suggested he would be my understudy, decided to move and join Middlesex. My idea was to sign a three-year contract but Kent stuck out for four because of the university commitments of the reserve-team wicket-keeper Stuart Waterton. The university commitments of other players have been a significant factor in my career!

What talent Paul Downton has, especially when standing up to the wicket. Mind you, he will have to look out because there is a crop of very fine young wicket-keepers in the country all pushing for an international place: players such as Bruce French, Jack Richards and Andy Garnham, who also has a lot of talent as a batsman. Robert 'Jack' Russell, who has enough ability to keep the talented Andy Brassington out of the Gloucestershire side, gets runs as well and, technically, stood up to the wicket he is extremely good for someone who has not been on the first-class circuit for long. If only one of them could bat to the standard of Geoff Humpage, the Warwickshire 'keeper – but maybe that will come to one or more of them. Paul Downton certainly showed in 1984 that he has the determination to become a batsman. I'm sure his batting could blossom and, if so, it would be difficult for anyone to dislodge him from the Test side.

After just over a month of the 1980 season I was back in the England side – what a surprise! When the news of the team for the first Test against the West Indies at Trent Bridge was broadcast on the morning of Sunday, 1 June, I was astonished. Ironically, Kent were playing the West Indies that day at Canterbury, where I was leading the side in the absence of Alan Ealham. It had seemed doubtful that the game's administrators in England would accept me back on Test duty – there still seemed to be some anti-Packer feeling, and anyway in the end I had not been picked to go to Australia the previous winter. I returned as the villain of the piece – not just because of my association with Packer but also because it meant that Bob Taylor had lost his place. He had never played against the West Indies before, and was never to do so, and he must have been terribly disappointed, especially after breaking the world Test record for a wicket-keeper by claiming ten catches in the Golden Jubilee Test against India in Bombay. It was a new experience for me to be the villain in my own country – that is how, I'm told, some of the media built it up – but of course it was nothing to do with me: the selectors chose the side.

My Kent colleague, Bob Woolmer, was also recalled; Chris Tavaré made his England debut, and Derek Underwood, although eventually omitted, was also in the England squad at Nottingham. Reporting to Trent Bridge, things had changed noticeably at England level. Ian Botham was captain, having undergone a tremendous change in stature since I had last played with him – from being the youngster whose international career was just starting, to being talked about as the leading all-rounder in the world. It was different for me, returning almost as a 'new boy' having not played Test cricket since 1977. England batted first, which was good from my point of view because it gave me the chance to get back into the feel of things, but when we fielded I dropped a very easy chance down the leg-side off Botham – Alvin Kallicharran was the lucky batsman. Because it was a simple chance, Botham questioned whether he had heard me swear. I am pleased to say that though rather disappointed at dropping such a sitter, I hadn't! Then I caught Viv Richards, not an easy one, but fortunately the ball stayed in my gloves after rattling around. If that had been dropped the Trent Bridge crowd, probably containing many Derbyshire supporters, would have given me a real roasting.

We should have won that first Test and would probably have done so if Botham and Hendrick had been fit enough to bowl flat out on the final day. The uneven-bounce wicket was ideal for pace, swing and seam, with conditions overcast, but it was left mainly to Willis, who bowled magnificently before the West Indies got home to a two-wicket victory. That was the first Test in which I played with David Gower. The second was the following year at Old Trafford against Australia, and each time he was dropped for the following match. In the second innings of the Trent Bridge Test Gower was unfortunate enough to miss a very difficult catch towards the end of the innings, off a skyer from Andy Roberts. The press didn't let him forget it for a long time.

The next three Tests were drawn and it was during the fourth Test at the Oval that we were asked to give a decision on our availability for the forthcoming winter tour to the West Indies. What an unfair time it was to ask such a question, bang in the middle of a Test match. All the players concerned had received a letter asking them to notify the authorities of their decision by this date. On the appointed day I telephoned Lord's to see if my decision could be delayed but I was told: 'No, especially not from you,' so I said that I wouldn't be available. I had asked if the decision could be kept private because it would obviously be very embarrassing if people were talking about me not going on tour while the Test match was in progress. Towards the end of the match, however, it was obvious that the selectors and Botham knew of my decision. Alec Bedser asked if I was sure about it and Botham was very upset. He was disappointed, he said, because he wanted to build up a side in which I would figure and was hoping that things would go better on the tour. I hadn't got runs during the series although I thought I had kept wicket pretty well. Touring certainly wasn't raised by the selectors when I was first recalled to the side.

So I was left out of the final Test, when David Bairstow replaced me. I had not really enjoyed my return to the Test arena, but possibly my lack of form with the bat had a lot to do with it. Commercialism had certainly come into the game, with promotions even taking place before a day's play and on the rest day. Quite a change from when I last played Test cricket. Commercialism, which had really been introduced by WSC, is vital to the game, but there is a time and a place for it.

On the field things were different too. I remember all the shouts from players. I was just getting down to keep wicket, to build up my concentration, when suddenly from the slip fielders came the loud cries of 'Come on, England,' 'Come on, Big Bob.' It was something which I had never experienced before and it is now referred to in the game as 'bubble' or 'rattle'. It certainly caught me by surprise. Perhaps my thoughts could have been a bit dated. It seemed out of place after a batsman had played forward and middled the ball to hear the cry, 'Well bowled!' It would not have encouraged me if I had been the bowler – quite the opposite: I would have felt that my colleagues were trying to encourage me because I was not bowling very well. The only time I would have wanted to hear 'Well bowled' was if I had genuinely beaten the bat. In my early days players tended to give you a quiet word of encouragement, which I think is much better. All this shouting seemed rather false, and I found it very difficult to get used to it. It must work for some players, and it has spread now into county cricket. Nearly every ball is preceded or followed by some remark or other.

As for my batting, I had never performed so badly in a Test series and I could not get out of the rut. I tried to go back and play as I had at Test level – defensively. I had not played that way for Kent since 1977, since I had been batting much more aggressively in the chase for bonus points or for victory in the second innings and in one-day competitions. With hindsight, I should have approached batting in that 1980 series in a much more attacking frame of mind. It was not until I got away from that series and analysed it that I realized how dramatically Test cricket had changed. Wickets had become much more inconsistent and the England batsman now had a much harder job, playing against fast bowlers nearly all the time.

When the Australians came to England in 1981 I gave little thought to the possibility of my playing Test cricket again. Paul Downton kept wicket in the first Test and was dropped. He had missed what looked like a straightforward catch, standing back, which happens to everyone, and it seemed terribly unfair to drop him. Bob Taylor took over for the next three Tests and England went 2–1 up. During the weekend that the side for the fifth Test at Old Trafford was announced we were playing Sussex at Eastbourne. Our cricket manager Brian Luckhurst phoned through to my room on the Sunday morning to tell me I had been recalled, and I thought he was joking. The decision really staggered me. Mike Brearley had by then taken over the captaincy from Ian Botham and it was very nice to be returning to play Test cricket under a person whom I had always rated very highly. Although I had very little warning of my recall I managed to attune myself better mentally for the prospect of Test cricket than I had done the year before. My mind was made up – I would bat as I had been doing for Kent, with a more aggressive approach, and it paid off. In the second innings, when my half century came up very quickly, my innings was ended by one of the best catches I've ever seen in cricket. I drove off the back foot at Dennis Lillee and the ball flew off to third man where John Dyson, sprinting round in the outfield, dived with his arm fully outstretched, and as he slid along the ground the ball just stuck in his hand. It was a once-in-a-lifetime catch and I remembered thinking as I ran to the far end of the wicket, 'It will probably go for four; no, he's going to stop it; oh no, he's caught it!'

During that Test Ian Botham really caught me out with one of his practical jokes. I had just caught Martin Kent, cutting at John Emburey, the Middlesex off-spinner. As Dennis Lillee came out to bat, Alan Curtis, who for years has done the Tannoy for Tests, made an announcement which I didn't hear. I asked Botham about it and when he said that it referred to some sort of record for Lillee, I started clapping because I could see everyone else was. Then Botham revealed: 'You've just obtained the record for wicket-keeping victims against Australia.' A voice from the crowd shouted, 'Stop showing off, Knott!' because I was clapping myself. Botham really tricked me on that occasion – fortunately with one of his kinder practical jokes.

Then in the final Test at The Oval, when we were trying to bat out for a draw and succeeded, I decided to stick to my new policy of playing my shots, and fortunately it worked. Ten years earlier if I had been batting to save a game I would never have played as I did at the Oval that day.

There was plenty to occupy my attention once the season ended because we opened the gymnasium that Jan was to run above our shop in Herne Bay. Jan involved in a gym! At one time that would have been somewhat surprising because I found it difficult to persuade her to do any exercise. Then in Sydney, during World Series Cricket, she went with Tony Greig's wife Donna to a gym and it was Donna who first sowed the seed in Jan's mind to open one of her own.

That was to give us a life away from cricket and a business for our future. Something apart from cricket – Jan has certainly given me that over the years. She has given me background encouragement with my cricket when it has been needed, and she has also given me complete relaxation from cricket with a totally different life away from the game. She has given me a home and a life that I could escape to when I needed. I would have hated Jan to have been waiting to question me about a low score or a dropped catch. We have had a wonderful life together, both in and away from cricket and we shall always remember the overseas tours we spent together, travelling the world on our own and with our son James. Jan for me was definitely heaven-sent.

The tour that winter was to India, and Keith Fletcher, who led the side, telephoned me and asked if there would be any chance of my going, but he knew really that my decision would be 'No'.

# Twelve
# South Africa

Plans for a tour of South Africa in the spring of 1982 came as no surprise to me. For many years there had been the possibility of such a trip, with one big company always involved, and harbouring the idea of taking some kind of representative side out there. Years ago I had been asked to sign a letter of intent stating that I was interested in such tours. Other players may have had similar letters – I don't really know. I took legal advice and was told there was no point in signing it, so I just made it clear that I would be interested without ever being aware of the detailed proposals, if there were any.

I had been to South Africa on only two other occasions, for double-wicket competitions in 1972 and again in 1974–5 before we went to Australia. Both were in Johannesburg and on the first trip we arrived three days before the tournament so we were able to get acclimatized to the altitude. On the second occasion county commitments prevented us from leaving for South Africa until the day before. Our flight was delayed and we arrived about 5 a.m. Five hours later I was keeping wicket in Johannesburg, with the heat and the altitude problems, and not enjoying it at all. I am a terrible traveller, especially when flying, and always take travel pills, which make you sleepy anyway and take a day or so to wear off. I was desperately tired and all I wanted to do was sleep.

*bove: Kent on parade. Ian Botham introduces Her Majesty the Queen at Lord's in
?80. Kent players are (left to right): Chris Tavaré, Derek Underwood, Bob Woolmer
id myself.* (Press Association)

*2low: Spot the ball! England celebrate the dismissal of Bacchus, brilliantly caught
? Botham off the bowling of Dilley at Old Trafford against the West Indies, 1980.
^hat a shame that Graham Dilley was unable to play against the 1984 West Indies
de because of a neck injury.* (Patrick Eagar)

*Ian Botham on his way to that awe-inspiring 118 against the Australians at Old Trafford, 1981.* (Patrick Eagar)

*As well as being one of the most popular players in the game, Clive Lloyd has proved himself one of the finest captains of modern times, leading by example with the bat and*

*Graham Gooch during his marvellous innings against the West Indies at Lord's, 1980.* (Patrick Eagar)

*Catching Martin Kent off John Emburey's bowling in the same match: my 100th victim against Australia. As well as being a very fine bowler, John is a great team man, always ready to practise. Not having kept to him a great deal, we spent many sessions in the nets together.* (Patrick Eagar)

*Above: In the early 1970s a computer selected this as England's best post-war team.*
*Back row, left to right: Knott, Laker, Bedser, Wardle and Boycott.*
*Front row: Cowdrey, Hutton, Bailey, May and Compton. Fred Trueman is the*
*missing player.    (Radio Times)*

*Above: With Leslie Ames (left) and Godfrey*
*Evans – a trio of Kent and England*
*wicket-keepers.*

*Left: Paul Downton, before he joined*
*Middlesex, was another who kept wicket for*
*Kent and went on to international honours.*
*Here he is preparing for a match in his early*
*Kent days.    (Photo Parrett & Neves)*

Keeping has its ups and downs, but can be a lot of fun, as Rodney Marsh and I demonstrate! *(George Herringshaw/Associated Sports Photography)*

*Above left: Great power and style fro*
*David Gower, as Javed Miandad tak*
*evasive action.     (Patrick Eagar)*

*Above right: Mike Gatting's 216 for*
*Middlesex against New Zealand at*
*Lord's, 1983, was the perfect answer*
*the selectors who had omitted him fro*
*the first Test two days earlier. He is a*
*batsman I would travel to see and is*
*fine leader. Will the England captair*
*come his way?     (Patrick Eagar)*

*Left: Allan Lamb on his way to a*
*hundred in the fourth Test at Old*
*Trafford in 1984. Allan's achieveme:*
*of scoring three centuries in a series*
*against the formidable West Indies*
*attack was outstanding.*
*(Patrick Eagar)*

*Left: Richard Hadlee, a great all-rounder, who in 1984 became the first player to achieve the Double of 1000 runs and 100 wickets in a season since Fred Titmus nearly twenty years before. It would be very sad if overseas players were no longer part of the county game. (Patrick Eagar)*

*Below: Two great friends and colleagues – Dennis Amiss (left) and Bob Woolmer. Dennis pioneered the wearing of protective helmets during World Series Cricket. Gary Sobers looks on while the white ball is on its way. (Left: Adrian Murrell/ Allsport Photographic; right: Patrick Eagar)*

*Jan and James – it must have been one of my better jokes. Inset: With Jan and James, enjoying ourselves abroad – this time in Holland with our Dutch friends Jos and Joke, and their daughter Annalie.*

There had been many reports throughout the 1981 season in England about tours to South Africa, but it was not until the final Test against Australia at the Oval that I was approached, in the England dressing room, about the tour which materialized in 1982. The plan apparently was for the sponsors to take an England team to South Africa at the end of the season or in the following March. The sponsors wanted the top England players to be available and they had included me. As England were touring India and Pakistan that winter it seemed that the tour to South Africa was to be arranged beforehand. There was a meeting in London after the season ended with Peter Cook and a representative of the sponsors. Cook was a South African businessman, who subsequently became the tour manager of the South African Breweries side. At that stage we knew that David Gower was not interested and the same later applied to Mike Gatting. What surprised me at that meeting was that Willis, Botham and Boycott were not there as I had thought that they would be. It was not a very successful meeting. The 'big three' were not present and it was made quite clear that the sponsors would only be interested if they got the full England team. The details at this stage were not very clear, although I knew that the timing had been altered, with the tour taking place after the England tour instead of before, to avoid problems. The fact that Willis, Boycott and Botham had not been at that meeting indicated to me that people were already getting cold feet. Indeed, I had had a letter from the TCCB and from Kent and quite realized that if I went there could be problems. Nevertheless, I did not appreciate that the reaction would be as extreme as it proved to be.

Meanwhile there seemed to be a difference in ideas between Cook and the sponsors. Cook was genuinely interested in getting a good side to play cricket in South Africa whereas the sponsors were only interested if it was the full current England side. I was the odd one out, having decided not to tour that winter, but the sponsors wanted me to play. There weren't any other meetings and it looked as if the tour was in doubt. The England players went off to India and Sri Lanka and I took a holiday in Scotland over Christmas and the New Year, giving South Africa very little thought. I didn't really think then that the tour would be on. It was well after Christmas when there was another telephone call from Cook, who had by then secured another sponsor. As I was the only player of the small group originally selected left in England, I was involved in many overseas telephone calls – Cook ringing me, and both of us ringing the England players in Sri Lanka. Boycott meanwhile had returned home from the tour in India and it was not known whether he would be fit to tour South Africa. I can remember ringing a hotel in Sri Lanka and asking for John Emburey, saying it was his uncle. That was the code by which he would know it was a call from me. On the first call, however, he didn't realize it was the code, and was very surprised when he heard me.

Cook said the tour could be on, and from Sri Lanka I heard that most players were going, although Botham had dropped out, in addition to Gower and Gatting. I had two meetings in London with Cook, one where I received a contract, which I signed after amending it with his agreement. Cook had rung up Saudi Arabia to speak to Mike Hendrick, Peter Willey and Wayne Larkins, there on cricket commitments, and all three agreed to go. But there was still a doubt about Boycott's fitness. The tour was to last a month and I could take my wife and James, which was ideal. I booked Cook and a South African solicitor into a hotel at Gatwick so that they could meet the England team when they returned from Sri Lanka and talk to them about joining the tour. Bob Willis didn't meet them, nor did Geoff Cook, and when these two dropped out it must have been bad news for South Africa, who were probably hoping both would be on the tour.

There was no stage when the tour was definitely on, so we knew it could suddenly be a big rush. In fact it was quick-fire action in the end. Peter Cook telephoned from South Africa to tell everyone the tour was on and a few days later we were on the plane. The players travelled up to London, met at a hotel in Knightsbridge and went by coach to Heathrow airport. We were ushered straight through into the VIP lounge; people were looking at us and wondering what we were doing. Nobody knew whether Boycott was going until the day of departure, when he just turned up and travelled with us. We flew to Johannesburg, arriving in the morning, slept in a hotel and, because of the limited time, were out practising in the afternoon. On arrival at the airport our story, if asked, was to be that we were just there for cricket coaching. Indeed, when we first arrived it was rumoured that the tour could still be off and we might all have to return home again. The squad was in fact of a very high standard, but the South Africans might have been interested in having a fuller representative team of current players. Later that evening there was an official press conference – photographs, interviews, the lot. I have never seen anything like it; it was top news. We knew then that the tour was definitely on.

Everybody realized there might be problems, but not to the degree there subsequently were. Some thought, like me, that the TCCB knew all the time that it was going to happen. It had been in the air during that winter and in the summer. The board had sent letters to players back in August 1981 containing mild warnings about what could happen to our careers, but my own view was that they did not particularly want to stop it – indeed that they welcomed the chance to test the reaction to sides from England playing in South Africa and might even have been hoping that it worked out well.

I had given the matter a tremendous amount of thought, having been associated with South African players a great deal throughout my career. When discussing the situation in their country, they would say, 'What do you know about it? You've never been there.' I had always been friendly with Stuart Leary, the former Charlton football manager Eddie Firmani, Bob Woolmer (who had been to South Africa coaching and playing for many years and whose wife Gill comes from Durban) and Tony Greig, and there were many South Africans playing with us in World Series Cricket whom I had known in England. From a cricket point of view I felt quite definitely that I should go on tour. It is a difficult problem and it would be nice if sport and politics could be dealt with separately, otherwise you could reach a point where nobody plays anybody at anything. Sport at least supplies a link between individuals and countries. I had always wanted to play in South Africa. It was the only country I had not been to on tour. I had been selected for a tour there once, but it had been called off – that was the year of the D'Oliveira affair.

My contract with the South Africans did not allow me to tell Kent about the tour, simply because the plans could have been passed on to everybody else if I had. I wanted to tell Kent, indeed I queried the contractual position, but in fact there was no problem with my county career, because the tour was out of season.

It was nice to see Graham Gooch getting the chance to captain a side at top level and the only alternatives in my view would have been Boycott or Peter Willey, who I had always thought would make a good captain of England. From the point of view of acclimatization the tour arrangements had all been too hurried. We really needed more notification of the tour so that we could have got fit and in practice before leaving home. Originally the plans were for one big Test match, with all the other matches building up to it, but suddenly they were cramming everything in to help the sponsors and I think that hindered us. To beat us, the South African team had only to play reasonably well early on in the tour, but if it hadn't rained in the last Test I think we would probably have won that. They caught us on a bad wicket at Johannesburg in the first Test, and went one up; if we could have drawn that it might have been a better series. Mike Hendrick was never really fit the whole tour, and I was certainly out of match practice, although Dennis Amiss, despite a similar handicap, played brilliantly.

The day before the first match of the tour a telex from the TCCB arrived via the deputy consul-general. It urged us to reconsider our position, outlining the chance of both India and Pakistan not coming to the UK in the summer of 1982. We really had no time to assess the possibilities of whether this would occur or not. The players certainly did not appreciate what was going to happen. Some of them thought as I did, that the authorities would have tried much harder during the winter to stop us if they had wanted to, particularly the TCCB. When I heard about our three-year ban from Test cricket, I was very surprised. I thought the outcome might be the same as it had been after World Series Cricket, where we simply weren't picked, but there was no doubt that Lord's got trapped into imposing the ban. They began to fear that other countries would refuse to play cricket with England. Having listened to both sides of the case, I could not really argue about the ban, although perhaps the words 'not selected' might have been better. Banning made us sound like wrongdoers. There was some discussion about whether we should fight it in the courts and there were plenty of firms suggesting that they might back us financially, but the decision was soon made not to go ahead, partly because it could have cost both the players and the game of cricket a lot of money.

I still feel that I made the right decision in going but I should add that I have always been anti-apartheid, and I certainly feel that to help that country people should go there. You might say that a cricketer visiting South Africa is a mere drop in the ocean, but every little helps. The more South Africans see and hear of how we live in other countries, the better. Being a Christian I cannot imagine a missionary saying 'We won't go there until apartheid is finished.'

Our tour of course led to the West Indian side going to South Africa, which surely must be doing wonders for the country. Just imagine young white and black children watching blacks and whites playing at the very top level together, either on television or live.

When I returned from the tour I attended a meeting of the Kent committee with Woolmer and Underwood. The committee made it clear that they were quite prepared for us not to play but were not going to sack us because it would cost them too much money. That was the committee point of view but the chairman, John Pocock, said that, personally, he wanted us to play. We were given a week off to think about it. I decided to play in the end because the feelings seemed to be mixed. There was obviously a split on the committee, with a slight majority in favour of us not playing. At least there was a split: when we came back from World Series Cricket the committee were far more united against us. At World Series time they were keen on developing and playing the younger players and, of course, they had Paul Downton then so it didn't matter too much whether I played or not. Now Downton had left Kent, so if I were to go it would leave them without an experienced 'keeper. Although the feelings about the tour in this country were mixed, there was no doubt that all the South African players were absolutely delighted that we went and so were that country's cricket fans.

What a pity it is that cricket fans all over the world have been robbed of the chance of seeing some of South Africa's top cricketers in action together, as a national side. At least in England, on the county circuit, Barry Richards was able to display his tremendous talent. He always gave the impression on the cricket field of being casual. During World Series Cricket, when I played with him for two years, I realized that this was far from the truth. He practised and trained with 100 per cent dedication, always continuing when others had finished. He could not have worked any harder at his fitness and you were always worried that if you agreed to throw and bowl to him in practice you would be there all day, because he just wanted to bat and bat in the nets. He was a fantastic player and the only thing that worried me was his hooking, because he tended to hook up. I roomed with him quite a bit in World Series Cricket and found him a very pleasant person. He astonished me with his knowledge of cricket, and he was highly professional. It is true that he had a casual appearance when he was given out – he just tucked his bat under his arm and walked off very briskly as if he had something else to do. He did that in county cricket and he did the same in World Series Cricket. I think generally this was his way of hiding his nerves. He got very keyed up to do well. His outward appearance hid his professionalism. He was a fine slip-fielder and a useful off-spin bowler too.

Eddie Barlow, like all his fellow South African cricketers, was highly competitive and confident, with a tremendous zest for the game. He was completely different from Barry. They both trained hard but Eddie openly showed how much he wanted to work at the game and how much he loved it. I would love to have played under his captaincy; he was one of the few cricketers who wanted to play every moment – he hated to see it raining. A farmer by profession, he was a fantastically talented cricketer, a really marvellous batsman. At the peak of his career, he played for the Rest of the World against England in 1970, opening the innings against Snow, who was a very great bowler then. Barlow was also a very underrated swing bowler, who always wanted to bowl – a terrific trier. I remember a tremendous spell he had at Headingley in that series; I was one of his hat-trick victims when he took four wickets in five balls. He was a very safe slip-fielder, a great fielder all round in fact. He was one of my favourite cricketers. Whenever you said 'Hello' to him, he welcomed you with enthusiasm. He transformed Derbyshire, turning them into a truly competitive side.

Mike Procter had enormous talent as a bowler, and was very quick at his peak. One of my most vivid memories is of him in 1970 bowling at Lord's for the Rest of the World against England in the first Test. He had long hair with a head-band. I went out on the balcony and saw this bowler up by the sightscreen for the start of his run-up. He set off like a sprinter, as fast as he could all the way. It was a fantastic, breathtaking sight. What an athlete. He was a very strong man, big, broad, very muscular, and like all South Africans he tried every inch of the way. As a batsman he was a wonderful player of spinners, being able to take them apart as well as any player I've seen. One of the biggest compliments paid to me as a batsman was when I was asked to bat above him and Imran Khan for the Rest of the World side during the first season of World Series Cricket. In Australia Procter's son Greg was a great cricket fan – there was never any complaint about children being on the scene at WSC and from time to time popping into the dressing room.

In 1977 at Bristol, playing for Kent against Gloucestershire, I drove a ball, swinging in, from Procter and edged it on to my left knee. As a result I could barely stand. He had been bowling quick on what was a rarity at Bristol, a quick, bouncy wicket. He said, 'You'd better go off,' but I said I would stay. I couldn't bend (I used to sway away from the bouncers in those days). He raced in and I began to play some shots, hitting him over mid-wicket with an uncultured shot which made him fume. As I couldn't avoid the bouncers I started hooking and got away with some unusual strokes. He kept bouncing me, about four or five times in one over, and umpire Alan Whitehead had to warn him. Then he said he would bowl off-spinners, but ran up and bowled more bouncers off a short run. I just kept cutting him over the slips. From this incident you might think we were great enemies but our families spent many happy hours sightseeing during those two World Series tours. Procter was also a very fine all-round fielder. I remember him catching me in the gully off Eddie Barlow at Headingley in 1970, a great one-handed catch diving to his right.

Ray Jennings has been the number-one wicket-keeper in South Africa for some years now. I first saw him when I was invited to take part in a double-wicket competition in 1972 and he was the other 'keeper. He was only a young lad then, but even at that age he looked a wonderful prospect. Something I have always believed in is the tall wicket-keeper and Jennings is over six feet. He was very quick and supple for a tall man, and when standing back he covered ground very easily because of his long legs. It is like watching Arsenal's Pat Jennings – he can dive full length to balls just inside the post much more easily because of his build. Ray Jennings was a highly competitive player and very fit, yet he will probably go out of the game without many knowing how good he was. It was a tragedy that he was not able to perform in the Test arena. He could have been one of the world's great wicket-keepers and certainly he is one of the best I have ever seen.

I remember Peter Pollock playing for the Rest of the World at Edgbaston in 1970 and for South Africa at Canterbury in 1965 against Kent. He reminded me very much of Charlie Griffith. He was not a quick bowler all the time but he produced many very fast deliveries.

Graeme Pollock, his brother, scored a double century against Kent at Canterbury in 1965. He is not one of my favourite players to watch, but what a run-getter. He has a very unusual technique for a top-class batsman – he likes to get forward a lot and when the ball is bowled short he often pulls or hooks off the front foot, or just as he is rocking on to his back foot. Whether he could use that technique against the modern West Indies' attack would be interesting. He used a very heavy bat, hit the ball very hard and has been a top-class player for twenty years. It is a shame that we have not seen him consistently at the top to confirm just how good he was at his best.

Colin Bland was a great fielder. What a fantastic display he put on at Canterbury in 1965 with a fielding demonstration throwing down the stumps for BBC television. It had been raining so the ground was a bit wet and slippery, but Bland held everybody absolutely spellbound. Eddie Barlow hit the ball to him and he came racing in on the greasy surface, picking up and throwing, seemingly in one action, and hitting the target almost every time. It was absolutely unbelievable.

Clive Rice is one of the more modern breed of top-class South African cricketers. In Auckland, playing for the Rest of the World against WSC Australia, Rice was hit in the ribs by Dennis Lillee. I was batting with him at the time and asked him if he was all right. He said, 'Fine,' and just carried on. We found out afterwards that he had a cracked rib. When training he sprints until he is nearly sick in order to get himself fit. As a batsman he plays straight, though he has a stiff-looking style. He likes to play on the off-side and hits the ball very hard. It is a great shame that, like Mike

Procter, he lost his fitness for bowling. The tragedy of some fast bowlers is that they just lose their fitness and have to rely more on their batting, though Procter, of course, bowled off-spinners as well. He was a big spinner of the ball, giving it a lot of air; the latter-order West Indians couldn't resist him in World Series Cricket and got themselves out.

Garth Le Roux, a gentle giant off the field, can look vastly different when running in to bowl. In 1979, during World Series Cricket, he was the number-one cricketer in the world. He was very quick and because of his strength and height could hit the deck very hard, making the ball lift and leave the right-handed batsman. As a 'keeper you always felt the batsman was bound to edge the ball to you or slip. Since he has been in England, playing for Sussex, he has also proved his worth with the bat.

South Africa has bred some great players and is still doing so. But if they cannot play regularly at the top level, will their standard drop away?

# *Thirteen*

# The Changing Game

One of the shining things about modern cricket is the ball itself. How important it is for bowlers if they can maintain that shine, and they have certainly learned the art. Whether the bowler works very hard at polishing it on his clothing or whether additives are used cannot be known by the umpires in all cases, but continual shine does enable the ball to swing about all day. When I first played county cricket, grassless, rock-hard wickets and brown dusty outfields soon tore the ball to shreds, with bits of leather hanging off. There was no chance of retaining the shine. But now outfields are lush green instead of brown, which helps to keep the ball new for much longer.

Over the past fifteen years or so there have been many stories about additives and there is no doubt that they have been used, and still are, at all levels. No one can prove it and, although I am against the practice, players have to accept it. I suppose if all sides use them the game is reasonably even, but it must give the bowlers a big advantage over the batsmen.

Lip-salve is probably the best known and most effective additive, but anything that's greasy has some effect – haircream, Vaseline, even sweat I'm told. Watching the modern bowler you can see his clothes stained with red marks, but how can you tell whether that is from shining the ball a lot or from using an additive?

The question of additives was raised during the series against Australia in England in 1972, when one of their opening bowlers, Bob Massie, had such success. There was no proof that any additive was being used – all I remember was that at the end of an over skipper Ian Chappell used to take the ball from slip, pass his fingers across his face and then wipe the ball, before handing it back to Massie as he was preparing to bowl. Massie swung the ball during that series as much as I've ever seen, with the possible exception of Gary Sobers. After the additive stories broke in the newspapers he didn't seem to swing the ball as much, but that could have been because he tired as the series progressed.

At Headingley in the fourth Test Peter Parfitt said during an interval, half joking, 'Let's get the ball. We're going to rush it down to the local police station and have it analysed.' That of course may be the answer – umpires could take the ball for a random check and send it away for tests. A system of spot checks could resolve the matter.

If additives are used now, it is very discreetly done, but there was a time not long ago when players might have had lip-salve in their pockets most of the time. Many use it correctly, as I do, putting it on my lips and nose during the intervals. I have never myself been able to have it in my pocket out on the field in case I landed on it when diving. There is a story about one player who had a metal canister of lip-salve in his pocket. He had used it a lot, so it was getting very low; when he put his finger in to get the lip-salve he cut it on the metal and had to leave the field for treatment.

These stories about additives have never been proved, but what is beyond dispute is the development by bowlers of the art of keeping the shine. The experts tell me that the best method is to shine it close to the seam and to ensure that the ball, including the seam, is always clean. In the modern game everyone helps to shine the ball all the time, whereas in the old days there did not seem so much emphasis on that and it was left mainly to the bowler.

Bonus points in the county championship have made three-day cricket more pressurized today. Every mistake made, even a misfield or a bye, might mean the difference between missing or obtaining a point which could cost a place in the table. Both sides are looking for a positive result, one chasing runs, the other pursuing wickets. Instead of the occasional scheduled early-afternoon departure from a ground for a long trip, it now seems more than likely that you will be playing beyond 6 p.m. With the rules introduced for 1984 dictating that 117 overs had to be bowled on each of the first two days and 110 on the third, it can be later still. The three-day game was played in a more relaxed manner at the start of my career. Pressure arrived at a much later stage of the proceedings if there was a win in prospect. There was not the thought that reaching 150 or taking the third wicket meant a point, and that stage can be reached very early on in the match. This makes for good spectator entertainment. I feel that the introduction of the four-day game would be hard on spectators: some of the most boring cricket I have ever played in and watched has been the Australian State games. In fact, entertainment value for spectators would be increased if the 100-over limit on first innings were reintroduced.

But to my mind the greatest entertainment of all would be to see English fast bowlers roaring in. We must encourage them. The only way England as a Test side will become highly success-ful is to have top-quality fast bowling. To that end we have to try to produce good wickets, ones on which they can learn and ply their trade. To get pace bowlers, wickets must be grassless, bouncy and hard, otherwise you encourage the medium-pace seamer (a type who will rarely win matches at Test level) and tempt the genuine quickie to reduce his speed.

The wickets must be flat, too, resembling a glass table-top. That way it will ensure that the young quick bowler will have to learn his trade properly, rather than getting wickets with the aid of uneven bounce. Let us not forget that with this type of pitch the contest between bat and extreme pace becomes fair. Another way of discouraging the seamer to the benefit of the quick bowler would be to go back to the old type of ball, which had a less prominent and slightly narrower seam. When I first started playing in Kent some of the wickets were the best I have seen anywhere in the world, of the type in fact that I have just described – Gravesend, Folkestone, Maidstone and Blackheath all fell into this category. At Blackheath there was a great example of the wicket being made up of rolled mud, that was similar in appearance to one I saw at Bridgetown, Barbados. There I watched some of the preparation: the wicket was flooded to give a muddy surface and the groundsman spun round a small hand-roller to churn this surface up with the edge. Then with old-fashioned rolling he could produce a pitch as flat as a pancake. I assume this could be done in England. If there are problems with the weather, the wicket must at least be shaved down to the grass roots before any rolling takes place. If you roll on grass I cannot see how you can consistently roll the strip flat. Of course, flatness is a matter of degree: I am talking of exact flatness, because the slightest undulation can make a world of difference to the contest between batsman and bowler.

What is more, these grassless, flat, hard, bouncy wickets would benefit the top-flight spinners. A really good spin-bowler likes bounce; in addition, of course, this type of wicket is always more likely to break up towards the end of the match. But any bowler on this sort of pitch will really learn his craft; the bad ball will be punished, line and length will be vital. In the 1984 season, as far as Kent were concerned bad balls frequently went unpunished because the standard of the wickets was generally very poor. They encouraged the type of bowler who should be discouraged in the game, the medium-pace seamer. Let the medium-pacer get wickets with swing.

I feel there are reasons for the decline in wickets, though I make no pretence of being an expert in the art of preparing cricket pitches. I mentioned rolling on grass; I think that another major reason has been the consistent use of the motor-roller. Most of these machines have two or even three rollers on them and one wonders how these can possibly be evenly weighted and balanced. If they are not, it does of course give a slightly different weight ratio from one roller to another which, in turn, makes it unlikely that the surface will be exactly even. The engine vibrates, and that must get through too. The combination of both surely gives a slightly wavy effect over years of continual use. Just as the old hand-roller, drawn by several people or a horse, has gone out of the game, so it seems have the flat wickets. Another theory I have heard put forward by my former Kent team-mate Bob Woolmer is that wickets are rolled when some parts are still damp and others have dried out. This too creates unevenness over a number of years.

I feel very sorry for groundsmen today. Although there have been directives that pressure should not be put on them to produce a result wicket, the unfortunate fact is that these days people seem desperate for a winner. The wickets should be controlled by independent officials; perhaps it should be the umpires. We had many cases in the 1984 season when an umpire could quite easily have said two hours before the start of play, 'There's far too much grass. I want it shaved off.' Counties have to be told that for the good of the game and to help us produce a highly successful England side we need good wickets.

But good wickets alone are not enough to bring on quick bowlers. They really could do with playing less county cricket. I would reduce the number of matches to sixteen or fewer. If it were sixteen, the counties would play each other once, which might also serve the purpose of giving cricketers regular time off, say two days a week. We play too much cricket in this country at present; players get stale and look to wet days for a rest. Cricketers playing abroad have better attitudes. They play less and so when games come along they are very keen to get on the field. When, however, county cricketers have sometimes appeared twenty-two days running, they cannot summon up the perfect attitude every time they play.

So my plan for the season would be along the following lines. Championship games (a maximum of sixteen each season) would be played during the week, with the Benson and Hedges Cup and NatWest Trophy kept as they are now, one in the first half of the summer and the other in the second. I would consider, however, the abolition of the zonal games in the Benson. They don't seem to bring in as many spectators as was hoped. At the week-end there would be the John Player Special forty-over competition and most certainly I would have another one-day competition. I would be tempted to look at a completely new-style tournament. It could take the form of three ten-over matches between two counties and be run on a points system, so that if a side were 2–0 down, there would still be a point to play for in the last match. It could be played on either Saturday or Sunday afternoons and I think the fans would absolutely love it. When John Player games now are restricted sometimes to ten overs because of the weather, anyone watching is riveted, including the players. They know something is going to happen off every ball. It might be wise to play this new competition on a Sunday, with bowlers coming off their full run-up because more time would be available. This would leave the John Player Special for the Saturday, when play could also start earlier and bowlers could again come off their full run-ups. Let's keep encouraging the true pace bowler.

This format, giving as it does less county championship cricket, might just attract more people to watch the three-day game. Provide too much and they tend to get blasé about it. And of course the main thing wrong with county cricket at present is that every day played means money is lost through the gate. There might be an argument for introducing one-day membership. At present the amount of cricket also lowers standards, because players get physically tired with being in action so much, and tired in attitude too, which can get through to the public. Too much cricket doesn't breed the right approach for Test matches. The Australians play only ten State games a season and whenever they turn out it is vital that they do well. County cricketers in this country are inclined to think, 'Oh well, if I don't do well today I've got another four innings this week!' Less cricket would alter that approach. In Test cricket you have five or six matches a season and you must have the attitude: 'I must do well in this match.' You cannot wait for the next game, because you might not be there. Overseas players, because of fewer games, have this type of attitude for every match they play in. However, no matter what is done with county cricket, I am not sure the public will ever come back in droves. They have got the one-day game now, after all, and that is the big draw. It is a fantastic spectacle.

When the Sunday League was first introduced players didn't altogether treat it as seriously as they might have done. That was certainly true of some counties Kent played and we were probably one of the first to realize how much one-day cricket was going to be part of our lives. That is probably what led us to the great success we had, and Mike Denness was largely responsible for this. We had won the Gillette Cup in 1967 but we then went on to win the John Player League in 1972 and 1973, won it again in 1976, took the Gillette Cup again in 1974 and also took the Benson and Hedges Cup three times, the last under Alan Ealham.

It is probably harder for a player to enjoy his cricket comfortably now, because there is not the time to relax. It is terribly draining mentally, much more so after a one-day game with the pressure of getting a result in the day, than after a day in the field in a championship match. It means that players have got to stay at a peak of fitness, which when I first started was not always the case. In the modern game there is no place for the unfit cricketer.

Pre-match warm-up exercises, mainly stretching, was very necessary for me; its importance was always stressed during the great days of soccer training with Charlton. I was taught to do it before undertaking any strenuous exercise. It is good to see that most cricketers loosen up before a day's play. At Kent over the last few years we have been extremely lucky in having our manager Brian Luckhurst, the former England opening batsman, in charge of practice. It is a pleasure to practise with someone as keen and conscientious as Luckhurst, who has arranged many sessions during the winter for me at the St Lawrence ground, Canterbury, through our much-respected groundsman Brian Fitch and his stalwart number two, Sam Fidler.

Outfielding in my early days was not as good by a long way as it is today, standards to aim for were not so high, and quite often it was not considered the thing to dive for a ball and get your trousers green. Stuart Leary always made a joke about it. 'Look, skipper,' he would say, 'he's greened his trousers,' and on several occasions players went off to change them. When the ball came gently towards him, Leary would jokingly dive in slow motion, putting one hand on the ground to stop himself getting grass stains.

Test cricket has changed dramatically too and as a spectacle has become far more entertaining. I have tremendous respect for the batsmen who were playing in my earlier Test matches, but again wickets were so much better and bowling attacks were not so consistently aggressive. Batsmen could play themselves in defensively, knowing that once they were really in the pitch would provide no worry in the way of seam movement (except on overcast days) or uneven bounce. I have experienced both types of wicket over the years and feel sorry for those who have never played on what was known as a 'belter'. Ken Barrington used to say, 'Book in for bed and breakfast.' And so often he did. When the bounce was even you felt you could duck short deliveries and they would fly well over your head; today you have to stay upright not knowing whether the ball will shoot towards your ankle or fly towards your chest. There is a greater element of danger, and batting techniques have been transformed. Batsmen play more shots, perhaps prompted by the poorer wickets and the generally better standard of quick bowlers as their pace has increased. If they play in a defensive way for a long period they take the risk of getting the unplayable ball, which might mean getting out having batted away for two or three hours for 30 or so. Therefore, the modern trend is to take up the challenge, play shots and in those two or three hours try to score something between 70 and 90.

I am not sure the public would accept a return to Test cricket as it used to be played, with defensive batting and probably three or four out of every five games drawn. From a Test point of view, England's batting tactics changed considerably against Thomson and Lillee. Players learned from their experience against those two. At Brisbane in the 1974–5 series Tony Greig cut high over the slips off the pair of them, so introducing a new regular shot in Test matches. Allan Lamb is an exponent of that type of stroke now; quite often he will move away to give himself a lot of room to cut the ball. Fifteen or twenty years ago that sort of manoeuvre from an international batsman was unheard of. It is a development that has certainly brought the public more entertainment. Take that Ian Botham innings against Australia at Headingley in 1981. What would have happened to England if he had tried simply to battle defensively on that poor wicket? He might have batted a long time for 30 runs or so, but Australia would have won the match.

I thought there might come a time when five-day Test matches would be dropped altogether, to be replaced purely by one-day Tests – and it could still happen. On England's tour of Australia and New Zealand in 1982–3 I felt as a follower on television and radio that there was more interest in the limited-overs internationals than in the Tests. And when England went to New Zealand and Pakistan in 1983–4 there were maximum attendances for the one-day games. But there has been a resurgence of interest in the five-day Test in this country since Packer and the professional cricketer has done a great job in spurring it and retaining public interest. Even in overwhelming defeat by the West Indies in 1984, England's Allan Lamb scored an unprecedented three centuries that would have won the admiration of any crowd. I would suggest that if we did get back to belting wickets and because of them drifted into the old defensive style of Tests, then one-day internationals would take over once and for all. But on perfect pitches I am sure the modern cricketer will play an even more attacking game in all forms of cricket.

Much has been made of slow over rates. Of course, the diet of fast bowling which I am advocating could decrease the over rate further. But it is something I feel the media have made too much of, whether in Test or county cricket. I really don't think the public notice it. In recent years the situation has become slightly farcical at times, especially in county cricket. Counties at risk of being fined for a slow over rate would take desperate remedies to increase it, with everyone tearing about madly. In a match doomed to be a dull draw at Taunton in 1983, Kent bowled thirty-three overs in the last half hour. This must be some sort of world record, but as you can imagine it was completely farcical, something the public noticed and would not have appreciated in normal circumstances. This is the sort of occasion when the public unquestionably notice the over rate – when it is dramatically increased for the sole purpose of avoiding a fine. If you went round the ground and asked spectators at any match whether it would make any difference if the West Indies bowled an extra over or two in an hour I don't think they would care.

There should be no minimum over rate at Test level. It is something that captains and umpires should deal with. Certainly over rates can become ludicrously slow. Take a Test in India when both sides were delivering something like nine overs an hour. Nevertheless a law governing the rate can affect captains and their policy; they can be forced to do something against their wishes such as bowling spinners when they are not necessary or asking a fast bowler to bowl off a short run. It lowers the standard of the game all the time. Over rates were kept high years ago because spinners were bowled a great deal more.

Looking back again into the past we have seen on television many times Jim Laker's great success at Manchester in 1956 when he took nineteen wickets against Australia. Laker was one of the greatest off-spinners I ever saw and I was lucky to study his great craft from behind the stumps on a Cavaliers tour. In 1956 the Aussies played him very badly compared with modern techniques. In those days on turning wickets the tendency was for bowlers to bowl away waiting to get wickets while runs were scored slowly. At Manchester batsmen seemed to play low, their bat well in front of their front pad. When playing forward they quite often lunged anxiously towards the ball. Today players tend to play high, with their bats behind the front pad, and allow the ball to come to them, rather than thrusting towards it. On a turning wicket batsmen take up the challenge and quite often one or two make 50 or so. The standard of playing spin on bad wickets is higher. I have already mentioned the brilliant innings by Rohan Kanhai at Gravesend on a rain-affected pitch just made for Derek Underwood. First ball he hit Underwood over the sightscreen and went on to make 107. Some players had to change their approach, like Mike Denness who was suspect defensively, but on a bad wicket at Bath took apart Somerset stalwart Brian Langford, something unheard of on that ground. Denness made 97 and 87 and those great innings transformed him. Asif Iqbal went after everybody.

I disagree with those who criticize the skills of the present-day player: I think they are different, but highly skilled nonetheless. To play Malcolm Marshall defensively, for instance, is much easier than when you need to score four or five an over to make sure you get a bonus point, or indeed to keep up a run rate in a one-day competition. That is difficult enough but an added problem in the modern game is that field placings are often very defensive. In one-day cricket this has been countered by fielding discs. I think there may also be room to bring in a regulation about close catchers in county cricket. They should always be in operation but when a new ball is taken the regulation should be increased for a certain number of overs. The return of perfect wickets which I am calling for might mean a lot of fast bowling, but the spinner, at least the top-flight spinner, could thrive too. England, I reiterate, will become highly successful only when we have top-quality fast bowlers and we will have them only when we get those wickets.

During my career there have been a great many changes, of course, and much of my fun out of cricket has come from analysing techniques – of batsmen, bowlers, fielders and wicket-keepers. I have really enjoyed experimenting in all departments of the game.

Take small wicket-keeping pads as an example. When I first

started playing 'keepers nearly always did their job with the same pads they used for batting, which soon led me to think they could be far too high and heavy. So I used smaller pads for wicket-keeping, and today the majority of 'keepers do the same.

Then there is the plastic finger guard. I sustained a broken finger at Canterbury in 1976, batting against Wayne Daniel. My return after that injury was two weeks later in the Test at Trent Bridge. It was a splintmaker in Nottingham who conceived the idea of the plastic guard, placed over my finger inside the glove. It didn't really work because I couldn't feel the bat handle, so later I experimented with the help of another splintmaker in Canter-bury. This time the idea was to place a plastic guard over the sausage-type batting glove. It proved very effective, affording fantastic protection, and now players like Geoff Boycott and Chris Tavaré use it.

Paul Downton, I notice, has been following my policy of using elastoplast on wicket-keeping pads. He employs it instead of a top strap, whereas in my case it is for the middle strap, which goes round the calf. Straps can be tight and very uncomfortable during a long day when your legs have to do so much work. The tape gives with your leg muscles as they move yet holds the pad in place perfectly.

During the latter part of my career I have experimented with rubber-soled shoes for batting and wicket-keeping. It's a great shame you can't wear them all the time because they are so comfortable, particularly for keeping wicket standing up. In India in 1976–7 I kept wicket for most of the series wearing rubber soles, but right at the end of the series it cost England a wicket. Sunil Gavaskar, hooking at John Lever, skied the ball, which lobbed up in the air. I started to sprint after it but fell flat, having slipped because of the rubber. Had I been wearing spikes I am certain I would have caught it and since then I have worn them. I was batting in rubber soles in Pakistan when Majid Khan, a fine swing bowler then, made a ball swing in very late towards my legs and as I went to move my feet quickly I slipped. Fortunately I just missed kicking down my wicket and the ball went off the front edge, just out of a fielder's reach, but that and an earlier incident were enough to put me off wearing rubber soles for batting. I was wearing them against Australia at Lord's in 1968, batting with Barry Knight. It had rained gently while we were batting and when Knight sent me back as we thought about a quick single I slipped over in the middle of the wicket and was run out by yards. Ken Barrington suggested in very strong terms that I should always bat in spikes, which I do prefer now because they afford a more secure feeling and are especially vital in the modern game. For keeping wicket standing back my choice is spikes, but standing up I would love to be able to wear rubber soles, especially abroad where the area around the stumps is rock hard and grassless. If someone could invent a boot with retractable spikes it would be ideal.

Another experiment of mine never materialized. After facing Lillee and Thomson in Australia in 1974–5, I purchased a baseball-catcher's face mask in Hong Kong with the object of trying to find a manufacturer back in England to do something with it for batsmen but I couldn't find anyone willing.

When I have retired and watch county cricket, it will bring back memories of the leg-pulling during my career. So many players have made remarks like, 'Those pads will do for my son', 'Knotty, you've got the game taped', or 'I'll buy you a pogo stick for Christmas.'

The day may well come when we have one man to run cricket, a cricket supremo. He must be a man who has vast experience and an abundance of enthusiasm for one-day cricket, for it is on one-day cricket that the game as a whole will increasingly depend. It would be marvellous if every county were financially self-sufficient and the only way apart from fund-raising is one-day cricket. It will stop the counties' dependence on the share-out of receipts from Test cricket. The post therefore must be filled by somebody who has a progressive cricket brain, for the limited-overs game has changed radically over the last decade, a process which will gain in momentum. He would be responsible for the whole structure of the professional game in England, deciding on the format of the championship and all one-day cricket. His duties would be purely administrative and I hope there would be time for him to pick and control the England sides. If not, another professional man would have to be chosen to do this. They would be full-time employees who are able to give their all to the job. That must be a lot healthier for the game.

Overseas players have been a touchy subject in English cricket for some years now, but I am all in favour of them because they have improved the game in this country so much. Looking at it as a spectator, because sooner or later I am going to be watching cricket rather than playing it, I would much rather have seen Lancashire in the days when Farokh Engineer and Clive Lloyd made them into such a very successful team. They transformed Lancashire into one of the greatest one-day sides in the game. But it has happened with many other counties. Mike Procter at Gloucestershire, Andy Roberts, Gordon Greenidge, Malcolm Marshall and Barry Richards at Hampshire, Joel Garner and Viv Richards at Somerset, Gary Sobers and later Richard Hadlee and Clive Rice at Nottinghamshire. My own county of Kent, for example, was vastly improved by John Shepherd and Asif Iqbal, who had a tremendous role to play in their glory years. All the other counties would probably admit the success of their overseas players – Essex with Ken McEwan, Keith Boyce and Nobby Phillip; Surrey with Sylvester Clarke and Geoff Howarth; Middlesex with Wayne Daniel, who really transformed them as an attacking side; Worcestershire with Glenn Turner and John Parker; Warwickshire with Rohan Kanhai, Lance Gibbs, Deryck Murray and Alvin Kallicharran (though probably Warwickshire never benefited as much as they should have done); Leicestershire with Brian Davison, Andy Roberts after he moved from Hampshire, and Paddy Clift; Derbyshire with Eddie Barlow, Peter Kirsten and John Wright.

Yorkshire, of course, have been the one side who have never had overseas players and just look how they've struggled. Since overseas players were allowed in English cricket, Yorkshire have won one competition, and that was a great surprise to everybody. It was just as well they had Ray Illingworth's cricket brain to lead them. Yorkshire seem to think mainly in terms of success in the championship and I feel that for the public that is the least important of cricket's four trophies to win. My order of merit would be the NatWest Trophy, the John Player Special League, the Benson and Hedges Cup and then the Britannic Assurance Championship. There was so much internal criticism of the Yorkshire side after the 1983 season when they won the John Player but most counties would have been delighted with that success because it is probably the competition that most helps to swell the takings of county clubs. Yorkshire's resolution in refusing to have overseas players has held back their progress tremendously.

Such talented overseas players as we have seen in this country immediately raise the standard in their county sides. That is tremendous for the spectator and very, very good for the game, because it gives young players more chance to play against great cricketers – a chance which, unless they reach Test level, they might otherwise never have. It is argued that the introduction of overseas players means that English players are prevented from reaching the top level, but if they have got the talent they will get into their county side and progress normally through into the Test team, as Bob Woolmer did from Kent.

A further benefit of having overseas players in county cricket is that it helps to bring their own cricket to an even higher standard. Nowadays you feel that New Zealand, India and to a certain extent Pakistan, although they might be weaker than Australia and the West Indies, are going to give you a very good game here. When I first played Test cricket you felt there was little competition against these sides. Although India did beat us in England in 1971, they should never have done so. We were winning two Tests when rain turned them into draws; then at the Oval Chandrasekhar had that freak match (taking 6 for 38 in England's second innings). I can even remember the West Indies struggling against England in this country. It wasn't until their players began to come over here for county cricket that the West Indies side really improved. They had two good series with Wes Hall and Charlie Griffith but there is no doubt that the experience their players had in England enabled them to become a very fine side. There was a change in their mental approach. Previously they had the reputation of not playing at their best under pressure, but once their players had the experience of county cricket they seemed to be able to cope much better when things were not going too well for them.

New Zealand have made tremendous strides in Test cricket in recent years, after their players had been over here and gone home to help in the development of their own country's talent: Martin Crowe playing for Somerset, John Parker and Glenn Turner for Worcestershire, John Wright for Derbyshire, Richard Hadlee for Nottinghamshire and Geoff Howarth for Surrey. If you went on tour in New Zealand a few years back you never thought you were going to lose – now you know they are going to have a good chance of holding you or, as we have seen, even beating you. The same can be said for other Test sides. Pakistan particularly have had players over here for many years and benefited from it – Mushtaq Mohammad, Asif Iqbal, Sadiq Mohammad, Sarfraz Nawaz, Javed Miandad, Imran Khan. As a result the side has made tremendous progress at Test level. India have not had so many of their players in this country but they have had people getting experience of English conditions, such as Bishen Bedi, Kapil Dev, Sunny Gavaskar, for one season, and Dilip Doshi.

Now the Test and County Cricket Board want to limit overseas players even further in this country and if that happens not only will we see a reduction in the standard of our cricket, but we could possibly see the international scene returning to the old days when New Zealand, Pakistan and India were of a much lower standard, with the consequent loss of Test receipts.

Since I first started playing county cricket the standard has risen tremendously and that has been due mainly to overseas players. Every county now seems to have at least one super-pace bowler, whereas when I first started playing it was a rarity to bat against an express bowler at county level. To play at Test level you have got to be a good player of quick bowling and if you are not getting very much practice in county cricket it cannot help your development. As a spectator I would feel robbed if overseas players were cut out of county cricket and the standard of Test cricket would probably drop considerably.

People argue that if there are two overseas players per county – and I think that should be the minimum – it means there are thirty-four English cricketers who might be out of a job. On the other hand there would be more money coming into the county clubs, which could enable them to pay for extra players, and youngsters would still have every encouragement to try and break into the game. Without overseas players the game could become so unattractive that crowds would be poor, media coverage would decrease and the result might be no jobs for cricketers. My plea is for these world-class cricketers to be kept and so sustain the great entertainment in our game.

# Appendix 1

# Alan Knott's Test Wicket-keeping Record

Alan Knott has 269 wicket-keeping dismissals to his credit in his 95 Test matches. They consist of 250 catches and 19 stumpings.

He has 105 victims to his credit in 34 Tests against Australia; 54 in 16 matches against India; 43 in 22 matches against the West Indies; 41 in 14 matches against Pakistan; 26 in 9 matches against New Zealand.

Knott has helped, or been helped by, 29 bowlers in reaching his tally:

G.G. Arnold 33; A.W. Greig 29 (27c, 2st); R.G.D. Willis 28; D.L. Underwood 27 (22c, 5st); J.A. Snow 27; C.M. Old 22; P. Lever 13; R. Illingworth 10 (3c, 7st); D.J. Brown 9; P.I. Pocock 7 (6c, 1st); M. Hendrick 7; K. Higgs 7; R.A. Hutton 6; N. Gifford 6 (4c, 2st); J.K. Lever 6; I.T. Botham 5; A. Ward 4; B.R. Knight 3; B.L. D'Oliveira 3; J.S. Price 3; J.E. Emburey 3; D.B. Close 2 (1c, 1st); R.M. Cottam 2; F.J. Titmus 2 (1c, 1st); G.A.R. Lock 1; K. Shuttleworth 1; B.W. Luckhurst 1; J. Birkenshaw 1; P.J.W. Allott 1.

**1 Pakistan** *10, 11, 12, 14, 15 August 1967*
K. Ibadulla    c Knott, b Higgs .......................................... 2
Saeed Ahmed    c Knott, b Arnold ..............................,...44

Intikhab Alam    c Knott, b Arnold ................................. 0
K. Ibadulla    c Knott, b Close ........................................ 5
Javed Burki    c Knott, b Higgs ...................................... 3
Hanif Mohammad    c Knott, b Higgs ............................ 4
Intikhab Alam    c Knott, b Underwood ........................ 16

**2 Pakistan** *24, 25, 26, 28 August 1967*
Majid Khan    c Knott, b Arnold ................................... 6
Wasim Bari    c Knott, b Arnold ................................... 1
Hanif Mohammad    c Knott, b Higgs ........................ 18
Saeed Ahmed    c Knott, b Higgs ............................... 0
Ghulam Abbas    c Knott, b Higgs ............................. 0
Asif Iqbal    st Knott, b Close ................................... 146

**3 West Indies** *14, 15, 16, 17, 19 March 1968*
G.S. Camacho    c Knott, b Brown ............................. 87

**4 West Indies** *28, 29, 30 March, 1, 2, 3 April 1968*
S.M. Nurse    c Knott, b Snow ................................... 17
D.L. Murray    c Knott, b Lock .................................... 8
C.H. Lloyd    c Knott, b Snow ..................................... 1

**5 Australia** *6, 7, 8, 10, 11 June 1968*
N.J.N. Hawke    c Knott, b Snow ................................. 5
J.W. Gleeson    c Knott, b Higgs ............................... 0
I.M. Chappell    c Knott, b Pocock ............................ 9

**6 Australia** *20, 21, 22, 24, 25 June 1968*
W.M. Lawry    c Knott, b Brown ................................. 0
A.P. Sheahan    c Knott, b Knight .............................. 6

**7 Australia** *11, 12, 13, 15, 16 July 1968*

**8 Australia** *25, 26, 27, 29, 30 July 1968*
A.P. Sheahan    c Knott, b Snow ............................... 38
R.M. Cowper    st Knott, b Illingworth ....................... 5
A.P. Sheahan    st Knott, b Illingworth ..................... 31
B.N. Jarman    st Knott, b Illingworth ....................... 4
J.W. Gleeson    c Knott, b Underwood ...................... 7

**9 Australia** *22, 23, 24, 26, 27 August 1968*
W.M. Lawry    c Knott, b Snow ................................... 135
I.M. Chappell    c Knott, b Brown ..............................10
K.D. Walters    c Knott, b Brown ................................ 5
B.N. Jarman    st Knott, b Illingworth ........................... 0
K.D. Walters    c Knott, b Underwood ........................... 1

**10 Pakistan** *21, 22, 23, 24 February 1969*
Saeed Ahmed    c Knott, b D'Oliveira ...........................18
Shafqat Rana    c Knott, b Cottam ...............................30

**11 Pakistan** *28 February, 1, 2, 3 March 1969*
Mohammad Ilyas    c Knott, b Snow ............................20
Majid Khan    c Knott, b Brown ...................................27
Wasim Bari    c Knott, b Cottam .................................14
Saeed Ahmed    c Knott, b Underwood ........................33

**12 Pakistan** *6, 7, 8 March 1969*

**13 West Indies** *12, 13, 14, 16, 17 June 1969*
M.L.C. Foster    st Knott, b Underwood ......................... 4
C.H. Lloyd    c Knott, b Brown ...................................13

**14 West Indies** *26, 27, 28, 30 June, 1 July 1969*
C.A. Davis    c Knott, b Brown ................................. 103
G.C. Shillingford    c Knott, b Snow ............................. 3
C.H. Lloyd    c Knott, b Snow ....................................70

**15 West Indies** *10, 11, 12, 14, 15 July 1969*
G.S. Camacho    c Knott, b Knight ................................. 4
G.C. Shillingford    c Knott, b Brown ............................. 3
B.F. Butcher    c Knott, b Underwood ..........................91
C.H. Lloyd    c Knott, b Illingworth ............................23
L.R. Gibbs    c Knott, b Brown ................................... 4
J.N. Shepherd    c Knott, b Underwood .......................... 0

**16 New Zealand** *24, 25, 26, 28 July 1969*
G.M. Turner    c Knott, b Ward ................................... 5
G.T. Dowling    c Knott, b Ward ................................. 4
B.F. Hastings    c Knott, b Underwood .......................... 0
R.C. Motz    c Knott, b Underwood .............................23

**17 New Zealand** *7, 8, 9, 11, 12 August 1969*
B.E. Congdon    c Knott, b Illingworth ...........................66
R.O. Collinge    c Knott, b Knight ..................................19

**18 New Zealand** *21, 22, 23, 25, 26 August 1969*
V. Pollard    st Knott, b Illingworth ..............................13
B.E. Congdon    c Knott, b Ward ................................30
B.F. Hastings    c Knott, b Ward ..................................61
B.R. Taylor    st Knott, b Underwood ........................... 4
K.J. Wadsworth    c Knott, b Snow ..............................10

**19 Australia** *27, 28, 29 November, 1, 2 December 1970*
W.M. Lawry    c Knott, b Snow ..................................... 4
K.R. Stackpole    c Knott, b Snow ............................. 207
A.P. Sheahan    c Knott, b Underwood ........................... 0
K.R. Stackpole    c Knott, b Shuttleworth ....................... 8
I.M. Chappell    st Knott, b Illingworth .........................10

**20 Australia** *11, 12, 13, 15, 16 December 1970*
I.M. Chappell    c Knott, b Snow ...............................50
K.D. Walters    c Knott, b Lever ................................ 7
J.W. Gleeson    c Knott, b Snow ................................15

**21 Australia** *9, 10, 11, 13, 14 January 1971*
K.D. Walters    c Knott, b Lever ................................... 3
A.A. Mallett    c Knott, b Willis ................................... 6
A.N. Connolly    c Knott, b Snow ................................ 0

**22 Australia** *21, 22, 23, 25, 26 January 1971*
K.R. Stackpole    c Knott, b Willis ...............................18
I.R. Redpath    c Knott, b Snow ................................... 5

**23 Australia** *29, 30 January, 1, 2, 3 February 1971*
W.M. Lawry    c Knott, b Snow ....................................10
I.M. Chappell    c Knott, b Lever ...............................28
K.D. Walters    c Knott, b Lever .................................. 8
R.W. Marsh    c Knott, b Willis .....................................28
W.M. Lawry    c Knott, b Willis .....................................21

**24 Australia** *12, 13, 14, 16, 17 February 1971*
K.H. Eastwood   c Knott, b Lever ................................. 5
K.D. Walters   st Knott, b Underwood ......................... 42
K.J. O'Keefe   c Knott, b Illingworth ........................... 3
D.K. Lillee   c Knott, b Willis ........................................ 6
I.M. Chappell   c Knott, b Lever ................................... 6
G.S. Chappell   st Knott, b Illingworth ....................... 30

**25 New Zealand** *5, 6, 7, 8 March 1971*

**26 Pakistan** *3, 4, 5, 7, 8 June 1971*

**27 Pakistan** *17, 18, 19, 21, 22 June 1971*
Aftab Gul   c Knott, b Hutton .................................... 33
Sadiq Mohammad   c Knott, b D'Oliveira ..................... 28
Asif Iqbal   c Knott, b Gifford .................................... 9
Wasim Bari   c Knott, b Price ..................................... 0

**28 Pakistan** *8, 9, 10, 12, 13 July 1971*
Sadiq Mohammad   c Knott, b Gifford .......................... 28
Mushtaq Mohammad   c Knott, b Hutton ...................... 57
Saeed Ahmed   c Knott, b D'Oliveira ........................... 22
Salim Altaf   c Knott, b Hutton .................................. 22
Asif Iqbal   st Knott, b Gifford ................................... 33
Wasim Bari   c Knott, b Lever .................................... 10
Asif Masood   c Knott, b Lever ................................... 1

**29 India** *22, 23, 24, 26, 27 July 1971*
G.R. Viswanath   c Knott, b Hutton ............................ 68
E.D. Solkar   c Knott, b Gifford ................................. 67
A.V. Mankad   c Knott, b Snow .................................. 5
F.M. Engineer   st Knott, b Gifford ............................. 35

**30 India** *5, 6, 7, 9, 10 August 1971*
A.V. Mankad   c Knott, b Lever .................................. 8
S.M. Gavaskar   c Knott, b Price ................................ 57
A.L. Wadekar   c Knott, b Hutton .............................. 12
S. Venkataraghavan   c Knott, b Lever ....................... 20
S.M. Gavaskar   c Knott, b Hutton ............................. 24

**31 India** *19, 20, 21, 23, 24 August 1971*
D.N. Sardesai　c Knott, b Underwood ..........................40
G.R. Viswanath　c Knott, b Luckhurst .........................33

**32 Australia** *8, 9, 10, 12, 13 June 1972*
G.D. Watson　c Knott, b Arnold ................................... 2
R.J. Inverarity　c Knott, b Arnold ................................. 4
I.M. Chappell　c Knott, b Snow .................................. 7
R.W. Marsh　c Knott, b Greig .....................................91

**33 Australia** *22, 23, 24, 26 June 1972*
J.W. Gleeson　c Knott, b Greig .................................... 1
R.A.L. Massie　c Knott, b Snow ................................... 0
B.C. Francis　c Knott, b Price ...................................... 9

**34 Australia** *13, 14, 15, 17, 18 July 1972*
I.M. Chappell　c Knott, b Snow ..................................34
R. Edwards　c Knott, b Snow ....................................13
D.K. Lillee　c Knott, b Greig ....................................... 0

**35 Australia** *27, 28, 29 July 1972*
K.R. Stackpole　c Knott, b Underwood .........................52
R. Edwards　c Knott, b Snow ...................................... 0
R. Edwards　c Knott, b Arnold .................................... 0
I.M. Chappell　c Knott, b Arnold .................................. 0
R.W. Marsh　c Knott, b Underwood ............................. 1

**36 Australia** *10, 11, 12, 14, 15, 16 August 1972*
G.D. Watson　c Knott, b Arnold ................................13
K.R. Stackpole　c Knott, b Greig ................................79

**37 India** *20, 21, 23, 24, 25 December 1972*
G.R. Viswanath　c Knott, b Greig ...............................27
E.D. Solkar　c Knott, b Greig ....................................20
A.L. Wadekar　st Knott, b Pocock ..............................24
F.M. Engineer　c Knott, b Underwood .........................63

**38 India** *30, 31 December 1972, 1, 3, 4 January 1973*
R.D. Parkar　c Knott, b Old ......................................26
E.D. Solkar　c Knott, b Greig .................................... 6
F.M. Engineer　c Knott, b Underwood .........................17

**39 India** *12, 13, 14, 16, 17 January 1973*
C.P.S. Chauhan     c Knott, b Arnold ............................ 0
C.P.S. Chauhan     c Knott, b Pocock ...........................11

**40 India** *25, 27, 28, 29, 30 January 1973*
E.A.S. Prasanna     c Knott, b Old ................................. 0

**41 India** *6, 7, 8, 10, 11 February 1973*
S.A. Durani     c Knott, b Pocock ..................................37
G.R. Viswanath     c Knott, b Greig ..............................48

**42 Pakistan** *2, 3, 4, 6, 7 March 1973*

**43 Pakistan** *16, 17, 18, 20, 21 March 1973*
Sadiq Mohammad     c Knott, b Pocock .........................30
Majid Khan     c Knott, b Pocock ..................................17

**44 Pakistan** *24, 25, 27, 28, 29 March 1973*
Zaheer Abbas     c Knott, b Gifford ............................... 4
Salim Altaf     c Knott, b Birkenshaw ...........................13

**45 New Zealand** *7, 8, 9, 11, 12 June 1973*
J.M. Parker     c Knott, b Greig ...................................... 2
M.G. Burgess     c Knott, b Arnold ............................... 0
K.J. Wadsworth     c Knott, b Greig ............................. 0
B.R. Taylor     c Knott, b Snow ....................................19
M.G. Burgess     c Knott, b Arnold ..............................26

**46 New Zealand** *21, 22, 23, 25, 26 June 1973*
J.M. Parker     c Knott, b Snow ..................................... 3
B.E. Congdon     c Knott, b Old ..................................175
K.J. Wadsworth     c Knott, b Old ...............................27

**47 New Zealand** *5, 6, 7, 9, 10 July 1973*
J.M. Parker     c Knott, b Arnold .................................. 8
B.E. Congdon     c Knott, b Arnold .............................. 0
J.M. Parker     c Knott, b Arnold .................................. 4
B.E. Congdon     c Knott, b Arnold .............................. 2

**48 West Indies** *26, 27, 28, 30, 31 July 1973*
A.I. Kallicharran   c Knott, b Arnold ............................80
R.B. Kanhai   c Knott, b Snow ....................................... 0
L.R. Gibbs   c Knott, b Arnold ...................................... 3

**49 West Indies** *9, 10, 11, 13, 14 August 1973*
R.C. Fredericks   c Knott, b Arnold .............................12
R.G.A. Headley   c Knott, b Old ...................................11
C.H. Lloyd   c Knott, b Underwood ...........................94
K.D. Boyce   c Knott, b Arnold ..................................... 0

**50 West Indies** *23, 24, 25, 27 August 1973*

**51 West Indies** *2, 3, 5, 6, 7 February 1974*
R.C. Fredericks   c Knott, b Old ................................... 5
L.G. Rowe   c Knott, b Willis .....................................13
Inshan Ali   c Knott, b Pocock .................................... 9

**52 West Indies** *16, 17, 19, 20, 21 February 1974*

**53 West Indies** *6, 7, 9, 10, 11 March 1974*

**54 West Indies** *22, 23, 24, 26, 27 March 1974*

**55 West Indies** *30, 31 March, 2, 3, 4, 5 April 1974*
C.H. Lloyd   c Knott, b Greig .....................................52

**56 India** *6, 7, 8, 10, 11 June 1974*
B.P. Patel   c Knott, b Willis ....................................... 5
S. Abid Ali   c Knott, b Hendrick ...............................71
A.L. Wadekar   c Knott, b Greig .................................14
G.R. Viswanath   c Knott, b Old .................................50
B.P. Patel   c Knott, b Old .......................................... 3
F.M. Engineer   c Knott, b Hendrick ...........................12
B.S. Chandrasekhar   st Knott, b Greig ......................... 0

**57 India** *20, 21, 22, 24 June 1974*
S.M. Gavaskar   c Knott, b Old ...................................49
S. Madan Lal   c Knott, b Old ...................................... 0

G.R. Viswanath    c Knott, b Arnold ............................... 5
B.P. Patel    c Knott, b Arnold ........................................ 1
S. Abid Ali    c Knott, b Old ............................................. 3

**58 India** *4, 5, 6, 8 July 1974*
S.M. Gavaskar    c Knott, b Arnold ............................... 0
A.L. Wadekar    c Knott, b Hendrick ............................ 36
A.V. Mankad    c Knott, b Arnold ................................. 14
S.M. Gavaskar    c Knott, b Old ..................................... 4

**59 Pakistan** *25, 26, 27, 29, 30 July 1974*
Zaheer Abbas    c Knott, b Hendrick ............................ 48
Asif Iqbal    c Knott, b Arnold ...................................... 14
Intikhab Alam    c Knott, b Arnold ................................ 3
Majid Khan    c Knott, b Arnold .................................... 4
Zaheer Abbas    c Knott, b Greig .................................. 19

**60 Pakistan** *8, 9, 10, 12, 13 August 1974*

**61 Pakistan** *22, 23, 24, 26, 27 August 1974*
Imran Khan    c Knott, b Willis ..................................... 24
Zaheer Abbas    c Knott, b Arnold ............................... 15

**62 Australia** *29, 30 November, 1, 3, 4 December 1974*
R. Edwards    c Knott, b Underwood ........................... 32
D.K. Lillee    c Knott, b Greig ....................................... 15
W.J. Edwards    c Knott, b Willis .................................... 5
R. Edwards    c Knott, b Willis ...................................... 53

**63 Australia** *13, 14, 15, 17 December 1974*
I.R. Redpath    st Knott, b Titmus ................................. 41
I.M. Chappell    c Knott, b Arnold ................................. 25
M.H.N. Walker    c Knott, b Old ................................... 19
A.A. Mallett    c Knott, b Old ......................................... 0

**64 Australia** *26, 27, 28, 30, 31 December 1974*
I.R. Redpath    c Knott, b Greig ..................................... 55
R.W. Marsh    c Knott, b Titmus ................................... 44
M.H.N. Walker    c Knott, b Willis ................................ 30
R.W. Marsh    c Knott, b Greig ..................................... 40

**65  Australia** *4, 5, 6, 8, 9 January 1975*
R.B. McCosker    c Knott, b Greig ................................80
I.M. Chappell    c Knott, b Arnold ..............................53

**66  Australia** *25, 26, 27, 29, 30 January 1975*
I.M. Chappell    c Knott, b Underwood ......................... 0
R.B. McCosker    c Knott, b Arnold ..............................11
I.M. Chappell    c Knott, b Underwood ........................41

**67  Australia** *8, 9, 10, 12, 13 February 1975*
I.M. Chappell    c Knott, b Old ...................................65
D.K. Lillee    c Knott, b Lever ...................................12
G. Dymock    c Knott, b Greig ..................................... 0
I.M. Chappell    c Knott, b Greig ...............................50
R. Edwards    c Knott, b Arnold ................................18
G. Dymock    c Knott, b Lever ..................................... 0

**68  New Zealand** *20, 21, 22, 23, 25 February 1975*
J.M. Parker    c Knott, b Underwood ......................... 121
B.F. Hastings    c Knott, b Old ..................................13
G.M. Turner    c Knott, b Lever ................................. 2

**69  New Zealand** *28 February, 1, 2, 3, 4, 5 March 1975*

**70  Australia** *10, 11, 12, 14 July 1975*
M.H.N. Walker    c Knott, b Snow ............................... 7
D.K. Lillee    c Knott, b Arnold ................................. 3

**71  Australia** *31 July, 1, 2, 4, 5 August 1975*
I.M. Chappell    c Knott, b Snow ............................... 2

**72  Australia** *14, 15, 16, 18, 19 August 1975*

**73  Australia** *28, 29, 30 August, 1, 2, 3 September 1975*
G.S. Chappell    c Knott, b Old ................................. 0

**74  West Indies** *3, 4, 5, 7, 8 June 1976*
B.D. Julien    c Knott, b Old ....................................21
W.W. Daniel    c Knott, b Old ................................... 4

**75 West Indies** *17, 18, 19, 21, 22 June 1976*
C.H. Lloyd    c Knott, b Underwood ..............................50

**76 West Indies** *8, 9, 10, 12, 13 July 1976*

**77 West Indies** *22, 23, 24, 26, 27 July 1976*
I.V.A. Richards    c Knott, b Willis ................................66

**78 West Indies** *12, 13, 14, 16, 17 August 1976*
L.G. Rowe    st Knott, b Underwood ........................... 70*
C.H. Lloyd    c Knott, b Greig .....................................84

**79 India** *17, 18, 19, 21, 22 December 1976*
B.P. Patel    c Knott, b Lever ......................................33
G.R. Viswanath    c Knott, b Greig ...............................18
S. Venkataraghavan    c Knott, b Lever ........................... 4

**80 India** *1, 2, 3, 5, 6 January 1977*
S. Madan Lal    c Knott, b Old .....................................17
P. Sharma    c Knott, b Willis .....................................20
E.D. Solkar    c Knott, b Willis ...................................... 3

**81 India** *14, 15, 16, 18, 19 January 1977*
G.R. Viswanath    c Knott, b Lever ............................... 9
S. Madan Lal    c Knott, b Willis ................................... 6

**82 India** *28, 29, 30 January, 1, 2 February 1977*
Yajurvindra Singh    c Knott, b Willis ........................... 6
K.D. Ghavri    c Knott, b Willis ...................................16
B.S. Chandrasekhar    c Knott, b Willis ......................... 1
B.P. Patel    c Knott, b Underwood ..............................17

**83 India** *11, 12, 14, 15, 16 February 1977*
B.P. Patel    st Knott, b Greig .......................................83
S.M.H. Kirmani    c Knott, b Underwood ........................ 8
A.D. Gaekwad    st Knott, b Underwood ........................25
* Record dismissal.

**84 Australia** *12, 13, 14, 16, 17 March 1977*
R.W. Marsh    c Knott, b Old .......................................28
I.C. Davis    c Knott, b Greig ..............................68
G.J. Cosier    c Knott, b Lever ........................................ 4
K.D. Walters    c Knott, b Greig ..................................66

**85 Australia** *16, 17, 18, 20, 21 June 1977*
C.S. Serjeant    c Knott, b Willis ...................................81
M.H.N. Walker    c Knott, b Willis ............................... 4

**86 Australia** *7, 8, 9, 11, 12 July 1977*
I.C. Davis    c Knott, b Old ...........................................34
G.S. Chappell    c Knott, b Greig ...............................44
D.W. Hookes    c Knott, b Lever ................................... 5
K.J. O'Keefe    c Knott, b Willis ..............................12

**87 Australia** *28, 29, 30 July, 1, 2 August 1977*
J.R. Thomson    c Knott, b Botham ...........................21

**88 Australia** *11, 12, 13, 15 August 1977*
R.W. Marsh    c Knott, b Botham .................................. 2
M.H.N. Walker    c Knott, b Botham ........................... 7
R.D. McCosker    c Knott, b Greig ............................12
I.C. Davis    c Knott, b Greig ..........................................19

**89 Australia** *25, 26, 27, 29, 30 August 1977*
D.W. Hookes    c Knott, b Greig ...................................85

**90 West Indies** *5, 6, 7, 9, 10 June 1980*
C.G. Greenidge    c Knott, b Hendrick ...........................53
I.V.A. Richards    c Knott, b Willis ..............................64
C.H. Lloyd    c Knott, b Lever ...................................... 9
C.G. Greenidge    c Knott, b Willis ............................... 6
S.F.A. Bacchus    c Knott, b Hendrick ...........................19
A.I. Kallicharran    c Knott, b Willis ............................... 9

**91 West Indies** *19, 20, 21, 23, 24 June 1980*
A.I. Kallicharran    c Knott, b Willis ..............................15

**92 West Indies** *10, 11, 12, 14, 15 July 1980*
D.L. Haynes    c Knott, b Willis ....................................... 1
A.I. Kallicharran    c Knott, b Botham ............................13
A.M.E. Roberts    c Knott, b Emburey ............................11

**93 West Indies** *24, 25, 26, 28, 29 July 1980*
S.F.A. Bacchus    c Knott, b Emburey .............................15

**94 Australia** *13, 14, 15, 16, 17 August 1981*
M.F. Kent    c Knott, b Emburey ....................................52
R.J. Bright    c Knott, b Botham ....................................22
G.M. Wood    c Knott, b Allott ...................................... 6
R.W. Marsh    c Knott, b Willis .....................................47
R.J. Bright    c Knott, b Willis ....................................... 5

**95 Australia** *27, 28, 29, 31 August, 1 September 1981*
G.M. Wood    c Knott, b Hendrick ...............................21

# *Appendix 2*
# Alan Knott's Test Hundreds

**New Zealand, Auckland** *5, 6, 7, 8 March 1971*
b Collinge ................................................................ 101

**Pakistan, Edgbaston** *3, 4, 5, 7, 8 June 1971*
b Asif Masood ........................................................ 116

**Australia, Adelaide** *25, 26, 27, 29, 30 January 1975*
not out .................................................................. 106

**West Indies, Headingley** *22, 23, 24, 26, 27 July 1976*
c Daniel, b Holder .................................................. 116

**Australia, Trent Bridge** *28, 29, 30 July, 1, 2 August 1977*
c Davis, b Thomson ................................................ 135

Apart from 5 Test centuries, Alan Knott has scored 30 half-centuries and a total of 4389 runs in his 95 Tests.

# Index

Aberystwyth, 68
Acapulco, 66
Adelaide, 3, 21–2, 45, 48, 74, 76, 90, 104, 108
Alderman, Terry, 36, 86
American All-Stars XI, 111
Ames, Frank, 12
Ames, Les, 11, 12, 17, 23, 29, 60, 78, 94
Amiss, Dennis, 52, 56, 57, 61–2, 63, 73, 94, 99, 103–4, 122
Antigua, 61–2
Arnold, Geoff, 10, 26–7, 64, 72, 74
Asif Iqbal, 27, 28, 41–2, 58, 84, 98, 104, 109, 110, 137, 140, 142
Asif Masood, 49
Associated Portland Cement Manufacturers, 19
Association of Kent Cricket Clubs, 17, 30–1
Athey, Bill, 39
Auckland, 47, 75, 126
Australia, 56–7, 98, 112, 130, 133, 136, 138–9, 141; 1964 tour of England, 14; 1968 Test, 35; 1970–1 tour of, 2, 20, 21–2, 36–7, 39, 44–7, 48, 49, 50, 54, 68; 1972 Test, 50, 129; 1974–5 tour of, 3, 28, 50, 54, 71–4, 75, 90, 97, 135; World Cup (1975), 82–3; Centenary Test (1977), 1, 62, 92, 93–4, 99; 1979–80 tour of, 4–5; 1981 Test, 116–17, 135; 1982–3 tour of, 135; World

Series Cricket, 4, 96–8, 102–8, 111
Australian Cricket Board, 111
Aylesford, 12

Bailey, David, 76
Bailey, Trevor, 17
Bairstow, David, 30, 115
Baker, David, 12
Bangalore, 52
Barbados, 26, 31, 62, 63, 130–1
Barclay, John, 36
Barlow, Eddie, 41, 124, 125, 126, 140
Barrington, Ken, 27, 29, 65, 134, 139
Bath, 137
BBC, 126
Bedi, Bishen, 92, 111, 142
Bedser, Alec, 5, 47, 98, 115
Belmont Primary School, 9
Belvedere, 9–10
Benson and Hedges Cup, 84, 110, 132, 133, 140
Bermuda, 6, 29, 64
Binks, Jimmy, 47–8
Bird, Dicky, 54
Birmingham, 82
Blackheath, 10, 30–1, 130
Bland, Colin, 126
Bombay, 53–4, 113
Botham, Ian, 39, 85, 114, 115, 116–17, 119–20, 135
Bournemouth, 36
Boyce, Keith, 57–8, 62, 140

Boycott, Geoff, 6, 21, 28, 29, 31–2, 37, 45, 49, 51, 62, 63, 71, 79–81, 100, 119–20, 122, 138
Brands Hatch, 88–9
Brassington, Andy, 113
Brearley, Mike, 4–5, 12–13, 23, 39, 60, 76, 99, 101, 116
Brice, Walter, 98
Bridgetown, 31, 62, 130–1
Brisbane, 36–7, 71, 73, 135
Britannic Assurance Championship, 140
Bristol, 125
Broadstairs, 12
Brown, Alan, 18, 21, 76
Brown, David, 33, 38, 41
Burge, Peter, 14
Burnett, Richard, 12, 56
Buss, Tony, 60
Butcher, Basil, 34

Calcutta, 52
California, 6, 66–7, 69, 109
Cambridge University, 12–13, 15
Canada, 67
Canterbury, 14, 18, 27–8, 36, 58, 65, 84, 90, 97, 113, 126, 134, 138
Cardiff, 14–15
Caribbean, 17–19, 28–34
Carr, Donald, 52, 98
Carreras-Rothmans, 17
Cartwright, Tom, 38
Catt, Tony, 12, 13, 17
Cavaliers, 17–19, 28–9, 57, 136
Centenary Test (1977), 1, 62, 92, 93–4, 99
Chandrasekhar, B.S., 141
Chappell, Bob, 20
Chappell, Greg, 45, 94, 103, 107, 108, 111
Chappell, Ian, 45–6, 71, 102–3, 107–8, 129
Charlton Football Club, 12, 21, 134
Chatfield, Ewan, 75
Chatham, 12
Chesterfield, 100

Chiswick, 50–1
Chittagong, 53
Christchurch, 46
Christianity, 66–70
Clark, David, 46–7
Clarke, Sylvester, 57, 79, 140
Clift, Paddy, 140
Close, Brian, 26, 27–8, 47, 65, 76, 77–8, 91
Compton, Denis, 68
Congdon, Bev, 56, 57
Connolly, Alan, 38
Constant, David, 12, 54
Cook, Geoff, 120
Cook, Peter, 119–20
Cornell, John, 100
Corsie, Eldin, 67, 69
Cowdrey, Colin, 2, 14, 17, 28–34, 39, 42, 43, 47, 51, 58, 73–4
Cowley, Nigel, 36
Cranleigh, 10, 27
Croft, 103
Crowder, Major Bert, 60
Crowe, Martin, 141
Crystal Palace Football Club, 21
Curtis, Alan, 117

Daniel, Wayne, 90, 91, 103, 138, 140
Daniels, 13
Dartford, 9, 12
Dartford Football Club, 88
Davies, Roger, 76
Davison, Brian, 40, 140
Delhi, 51–2, 92
Denness, Mike, 28, 41–2, 51, 58, 60, 62, 73, 74, 83–4, 110, 133, 137
Derby, 100
Derbyshire, 100, 114, 124, 140, 141
Dev, Kapil, 142
Dexter, Ted, 83
Dilley, Graham, 80
Dixon, Alan, 18
D'Oliveira, Basil, 20, 26, 27, 30, 38, 45, 51, 121
Doshi, Dilip, 142

Dover, 14, 88
Downton, Paul, 4, 8, 109–11, 112–13, 116, 123, 138
Dujon, Jeff, 19
Dye, 42
Dymock, Geoff, 74
Dyson, John, 76, 116

Ealham, Alan, 12, 22, 28, 42–2, 58, 67, 110, 113, 133
East Africa, 82
East Molesey, 30
Eastbourne, 116
Edgbaston, 18, 28, 49, 82, 83, 126
Edmonds, Phil, 16
Edrich, John, 29, 47, 51, 73, 78, 91
Edwards, Mike, 77
Edwards, Ross, 72
Edwards, Wally, 71
Elliott, Charlie, 47, 99
Elms, Richard, 89
Eltham Baths, 9, 11, 54
Emburey, John, 51, 76, 116, 120
Engineer, Farokh, 41, 140
Erith, 8, 12
Erith Technical College Association, 9–10
Essex, 13, 25, 42, 43, 57, 92, 140
Essex schools, 83
Evans, David, 40, 101
Evans, Godfrey, 17–18, 27, 87, 91
Exeter University, 8

FA Cup, 21
Featherstone, Norman, 50–1
Fidler, Sam, 134
Fillary, Ted, 16–17
Firmani, Eddie, 121
Fitch, Brian, 134
Fletcher, Keith, 1, 17, 52, 56, 57, 64, 72, 74, 77, 117
Fletcher, Sue, 1
Folkestone, 12, 13, 60, 130
Fowler, George, 31
Fredericks, Roy, 63
French, Bruce, 113

Garner, Joel, 103, 140
Garnham, Andy, 113
Gatting, Mike, 119–20
Gavaskar, Sunil, 59, 138, 142
Georgetown, Guyana, 33–4, 64
Ghavri, Karsan, 93
Gibbs, Lance, 31, 34, 41, 64, 140
Gillette Cup, 28, 51, 65, 133
Gilmour, Gary, 57, 82–3
Glamorgan, 18, 40, 47
Gleeson, John, 36–7
Gloucestershire, 13, 39, 113, 125, 140
Gomes, Larry, 51
Gooch, Graham, 83, 122
Gower, David, 114, 119–20
Graham, Norman, 12, 42
Graveney, Tom, 17, 29
Graves, Peter, 10
Gravesend, 18, 58, 76, 130, 137
Greenidge, Gordon, 103, 140
Greig, Donna, 117
Greig, Tony, 4, 50, 52, 53, 61, 63–4, 71, 72–3, 82, 84–5, 89, 91–3, 96–104, 111, 121, 135
Griffith, Billy, 59
Griffith, Charlie, 26, 33, 126, 141
Griffith, Mike, 59
Grout, Wally, 14, 65
Guyana, 33–4, 64

Hadlee, Richard, 140, 141
Hall, Wes, 26, 33, 141
Hampshire, 36, 140
Hampshire, Jackie, 17, 18, 40
Hanif Mohammad, 27
Hastings, 36
Hawaii, 6
Hawke, Neil, 40
Haynes, Desmond, 106
Headingley, 40, 41, 49, 64, 82, 91, 93, 99, 124, 125, 129, 135
Headley, Ron, 17
Heathrow airport, 29, 120
Hendrick, Mike, 71, 100, 114, 120, 122
Hendricks, Jackie, 18–19
Herne Bay, 22, 60, 110, 117

Hesketh Park, 9
Higgs, Ken, 25, 26
Hills, Richard, 41
Holding, Michael, 91–2, 103, 104
Holford, David, 31
Hong Kong, 6, 139
Hookes, David, 111
Howarth, Geoff, 140, 141
Humpage, Geoff, 113
Hutton, Sir Leonard, 13
Hutton, Richard, 13

Ibadulla, Billy, 25, 27, 77–8
Illingworth, Ray, 14, 39, 40, 44–7, 49–51, 56, 59, 60, 68, 99, 140
Imran Khan, 49, 103, 104, 105, 125, 142
India, 1, 3, 6, 26, 28, 49, 59, 64, 71, 98, 117, 119, 122, 136, 141, 142; Golden Jubilee Test, 113; 1972–3 tour of, 51–4, 99; 1974 Test, 66; 1976–7 tour of, 65, 92–3, 138
Inman, Clive, 13
Inshan Ali, 31
Insole, Doug, 98
International Cavaliers, 17–19, 28–9, 57, 136
International Cricket Conference, 102, 111
Intikhab Alam, 28, 49

Jamaica, 29, 34, 61, 63
Jameson, John, 82
Jarvis, 42
Javed Miandad, 142
Jenner, Terry, 71, 74
Jennings, Pat, 126
Jennings, Ray, 11, 125–6
Johannesburg, 118, 120, 122
John Player Special League, 51, 65, 84, 132–3, 140
Johnson, Graham, 42, 58, 64
Johnson, Marion, 64
Johnson's Leap, 64
Jones, Eifion, 47

Jones, Jeff, 30, 33, 34
Jones, Reg, 20
Julien, Bernard, 41–2, 58, 60–1, 100

Kaiatura Falls, 64
Kallicharran, Alvin, 60–1, 63, 114, 140
Kanhai, Rohan, 40, 41, 58, 137, 140
Karachi, 38
Kensington Temple, 67, 68–9
Kent, Martin, 116
Kent and Canterbury hospital, 82
Kent County Cricket Club, 9, 10, 42–3, 60; AK joins staff of, 11–12; AK joins first eleven, 1–13; win county championship, 41–2; win John Player League, 51, 84; win Gillette Cup, 65; AK's benefit year, 86–8; AK resigns from, 109–10; recall AK, 110–11, 112; reactions to AK's visit to South Africa, 123; overseas players, 140
Kerslake, Roy, 13
Kingston, Jamaica, 31, 61
Kippins, 34
Kirsten, Peter, 140
Knight, Barry, 40, 138–9
Knott, Eric (AK's father), 8–9, 10–11
Knott, Francis (AK's brother), 9
Knott, James (AK's son), 3, 7, 19, 82, 107, 120
Knott, Jan (AK's wife), 1–4, 7, 19, 22, 60, 64, 66–9, 82, 89, 92, 97, 107, 117, 120
Knott, Margaret (AK's mother), 9, 31, 83

Laker, Jim, 17, 136
Lamb, Allan, 73, 135
Lancashire, 21, 40, 65, 72, 76, 140
Landau, Max, 21
Langford, Brian, 137
Larkins, Wayne, 120

Latchman, Harry, 51
Lawry, Bill, 14, 37
Le Roux, Garth, 36, 103, 127
Leadbeater, Barry, 54
Leary, Stuart, 12, 76, 121, 134
Leeds, 39
Leicestershire, 13, 40, 45, 47, 60, 140
*Let's Play Cricket*, 42
Lever, John, 57, 92, 138
Lever, Peter, 21, 71, 74, 75
Lewis, Claude, 11, 15
Lewis, Tony, 52, 53, 99
Lillee, Dennis, 3, 36, 50, 54, 71–5, 78, 93, 103, 106, 107, 116–17, 126, 135, 139
Linden Park, 30
Lloyd, Clive, 41, 61, 63, 140
Lloyd, David, 72
Lobo, Dr, 26
Lock, Tony, 34, 47
Long, Arnold, 51
Lord's, 16–17, 20, 28, 37–8, 56, 64–5, 91, 98, 138–9
Luckhurst, Brian, 12, 21, 37, 42, 58, 116, 134

McEwan, Ken, 140
Madras, 52, 53, 92
Maidstone, 51, 130
Majid Khan, 23, 78, 138
Majorca, 38
Mallett, Ashley, 57, 74
Manchester, 136–7
Margate Football Club, 88
Marsh, Rodney, 37, 44–5, 48, 72, 83, 93, 94–5, 103, 105, 107–8
Marshall, Malcolm, 54, 137, 140
Martin-Jenkins, Christopher, 42
Massie, Bob, 129
May, Peter, 10, 27
MCC, 28, 35, 49, 97
Melbourne, 1, 37, 73–4, 92, 94, 104, 105, 107, 108
Melville, Jimmy, 10
Middlesex, 17, 20, 43, 50–1, 98, 112, 140
Miller, Keith, 99

Mitcham, 21
Morris, Jack, 9
Mote Park, 51
Murray, David, 19
Murray, Deryck, 19, 106, 140
Murray, John, 25–6, 47
Mushtaq Mohammad, 27, 38, 41, 142

NatWest Trophy, 43, 132, 140
New York, 111
New Zealand, 6, 39, 59, 98, 141–2; 1970–1 tour of, 46, 47, 49; 1973 Test match, 56; 1974–5 tour of, 74–5; 1982–3 tour of, 135; 1983–4 tour of, 135
Newfoundland, 29
Nore Command, 12
Northamptonshire, 12, 13, 76, 85–6
Northumberland Heath Secondary Modern School, Erith, 8
Nottingham, 114, 138
Nottinghamshire, 112, 141

Old, Chris, 53
Old Trafford, 38, 78, 91, 99, 114, 116
Olten, Mike, 10
O'Neill, Norman, 14
O'Reilly, Bill, 39
Ormrod, Alan, 53
Oval, 28, 35, 39, 54, 106, 117

Packer, Kerry, 4, 96, 98, 100–1, 109, 111, 113, 135
Padmore, Albert, 90
Page, Colin, 11, 12
Pakistan, 30, 49, 71, 96, 98, 119, 122, 138, 141, 142; MCC under-25 tour of (1966), 23–4, 28, 53; 1967 Test, 25–7; 1969 tour of, 2, 38–9, 57; 1971 Test match, 49; 1972–3 tour of, 51, 52; 1973 Test, 64–5; 1974 Test, 66; 1983–4 tour of, 135

Parfitt, Peter, 129
Parker, John, 140, 141
Parks, Jim, 29–30, 31, 34, 47, 59
Pascoe, 103
PBL Sports Ltd, 111
Perth, 71, 73, 94, 103, 104
Peshawar, 23
Phebey, Arthur, 110, 112
Phillip, Nobby, 140
Pocock, John, 109, 112, 123
Pocock, Pat, 34, 63
Pollock, Graeme, 41, 126
Pollock, Peter, 126
Pook, Alan (AK's brother-in-law), 60
Pook, Brian (AK's brother-in-law), 20, 68
Pook, Graham (AK's brother-in-law), 19–20
Pook, Linda (BP's wife), 68
Pook, Linda (AP's wife), 60
Pope, George, 31
Port of Spain, 29–30, 60–1
Presdee, Jim, 15
Pritchard, Graham, 13
Procter, Greg, 125
Procter, Mike, 41, 102, 103, 124–5, 127, 140
Prodger, John, 12, 14–15, 88
Prodger, Margaret, 88

Randall, Derek, 93–4
Redpath, Ian, 14, 50
Revell, Charlie, 21
Rice, Clive, 103, 126–7, 140
Richards, Barry, 41, 106–7, 111, 123–4, 140
Richards, Jack, 113
Richards, Viv, 18, 51, 62, 90–1, 103, 114, 140
Richardson, Peter, 14–15
Roberts, Andy, 63, 91, 103, 104, 111, 114, 140
Robinson, Richie, 11
Rodriguez, Willie, 16, 31
Rogers, Andy, 69
Rowe, Lawrence, 63, 91
Royal Engineers, 12

Royal Homeopathic Hospital, London, 20
Russell, Eric, 26
Russell, Robert 'Jack', 113

Sabina Park, 18
Sadiq Mohammad, 142
St Lawrence ground, Canterbury, 134
San Francisco, 6
Sang Hue, Douglas, 60–1
Sarfraz Nawaz, 142
Saudi Arabia, 120
Sayer, David, 12, 13
Scotland, 119
Scott, Malcolm, 12
Selvey, Mike, 51, 91
Severn, Barbara, 67
Severn, Billy, 67–8, 69
Severn, Dr Clifford, 66, 67
Sharpe, Phil, 40
Shea Stadium, New York, 111
Sheahan, Paul, 56–7
Sheffield, 80
Sheffield Shield, 40
Shelley, Billy, 66–7
Shelley, Roy, 66–7
Shelley, Vonnie, 66–7
Shepherd, John, 41–2, 58, 64, 140
Simmons, Jack, 40
Smith, C. Aubrey, 67
Snow, John, 5–6, 28, 33, 34, 44, 51, 59, 74, 89, 91, 102, 124
Sobers, Gary, 18, 31, 32, 34, 40, 41, 58, 63, 64, 111, 129, 140
Somerset, 13, 43, 65, 137, 140, 141
South Africa, 17, 38, 40, 48, 57, 61, 67, 70, 96, 98, 118–27
South African Breweries, 119
South of England Schools, 10, 27
SPARKS, 88
Sri Lanka, 1, 119, 120
Stackpole, Keith, 94
Steele, David, 85–6, 91
Stewart, Mickey, 77
Stokoe, Bob, 21
*Sunday Express*, 68

Sunday League, 133
Sunderland Football Club, 21
Surrey, 30, 51, 57, 77, 140, 141
Sussex, 12, 59, 89, 96–7, 116, 127
Swanley, 50
Swanton, Jim, 14
Swarbrook, Fred, 100
Sydney, 6–7, 44, 45, 54, 72, 74, 90, 103, 105, 107, 109, 117

Taj Mahal, 6
Tasmania, 2, 6, 40, 49
Taunton, 136
Tavaré, Chris, 30, 42–3, 51, 113, 138
Taylor, Bob, 45–8, 63, 90, 100, 113, 116
Taylor, Chris, 90
Test and County Cricket Board (TCCB), 1–3, 97, 98, 101, 102, 119, 121, 122, 142
Thomas, Bernard, 3, 20, 21, 75, 90, 106
Thomson, Jeff, 3, 71–5, 78, 92, 135, 139
Titmus, Fred, 26, 30, 74, 90
Tolchard, Roger, 47, 90, 92
Tooting, 21
Trent Bridge, 19, 25, 28, 37, 47, 54, 90, 113–14, 138
Trinidad, 31–2, 63–4
Trueman, Fred, 17, 28
Tucker, Bill, 20
Tunbridge Wells, 12, 13, 31, 80
Turner, Glenn, 140, 141

Ufton, Derek, 12, 21
Underwood, Derek, 10, ʼ13, 16, 20, 26–7, 28, 33, 35–6, 40, 42, 44–5, 47, 52–3, 58, 60, 63–4, 65, 74, 78, 91, 98, 107, 109, 113–14, 123, 137
United States of America, 66–7, 69, 111

Wadekar, Ajit, 53
Wales, 68
Walker, Max, 72, 74

Walter Lawrence Trophy, 97
Walters, Doug, 71, 74
Warwickshire, 28, 58, 113, 140
Wasim Bari, 38, 49, 65
Waterton, Stuart, 113
Welham, Dirk, 39
Wellingborough, 13
Wembley, 21
West Indies, 5, 51, 78, 84, 86, 96, 99, 127, 135, 136, 141; International Cavaliers tour of, 17–19; 1966 tour of, 18; 1967–8 tour of, 28–34, 41; 1969 Test match, 39, 40; 1973 Test match, 57–60; 1973–4 tour of, 2, 49, 60–4, 71; World Cup (1975), 83; 1976 Test, 90–2; 1980 Test, 54, 113–15; tour of South Africa, 123; World Series Cricket, 106
White, 'Butch', 18
Whitehead, Alan, 54, 125
Willey, Peter, 91, 120, 122
Willis, Bob, 46, 71, 74, 92, 100–1, 114, 119, 120
Wills, Roy, 10
Windows, Tony, 13
Wisden, 39
Wood, Barry, 53
Wooller, Wilf, 14–15
Woolley, Frank, 12, 56
Woolmer, Bob, 41–2, 58, 62, 88, 92, 100, 109, 113, 121, 123, 131, 141
Woolmer, Gill, 121
Worcester, 11, 65
Worcestershire, 15, 140, 141
World Cup (1975), 82–3
World Series Cricket, 3, 4, 11, 23, 48, 58, 70, 76, 80, 93–5, 96–108, 109–12, 115, 117, 121–5, 127
Wright, John, 140, 141

Yorkshire, 13, 14, 27–8, 39, 45, 80, 140

Zaheer Abbas, 49